I0616316

Tamara's Journey THROUGH Trials AND Tears

Tamara's Journey THROUGH Trials AND Tears

TAMARA RIVERA

Copyright © 2025 by Tamara Rivera

All rights reserved. No part of this publication may be reproduced, distributed, or transmitted in any form or by any means, including photocopying, recording, or other electronic or mechanical methods, without the prior written permission of the author, except in the case of brief quotations embodied in critical reviews and certain other noncommercial uses permitted by copyright law.

Printed in the United States of America

ISBN 979-8-89114-148-3 (hc)
ISBN 979-8-89114-147-6 (sc)
ISBN 979-8-89114-149-0 (e)

Library of Congress Control Number: 2024925510

2025.02.21

MainSpring Books
5901 W. Century Blvd
Suite 750
Los Angeles, CA, US, 90045

www.mainspringbooks.com

My Early Life

I was born in 1962, on a warm Puerto Rican morning. My proud parents welcomed me as their second child and firstborn son. For the first year of my life, I lived in Puerto Rico. However, my parents moved to Chicago, Illinois, and bought a home there. During that first year, I stayed with my aunt Lydia in Puerto Rico.

In 1963, my aunt Lydia joined my parents in Illinois, and we lived there until I turned ten. It was in Chicago, IL that I attended a Catholic school. Growing up, one of my earliest memories of feeling different occurred when I was five years old.

During my childhood in Chicago, I had a wonderful time. For the next nine years of my childhood, I grew up like any normal boy, discovering fresh adventures in my parents' home. Like most boys at that time, my first toys were a baseball bat and a red wagon. The sight of an old, rusted 1930s Ford in my dad's garage that truly caught my attention. Despite my love for the city, I couldn't stand Chicago's brutal cold. Then, in the early '70s, my parents moved back to Puerto Rico. Unfortunately, I didn't know any Spanish, and this became a major struggle for me in school.

Learning Spanish was challenging during the move back to Puerto Rico, as my parents didn't prioritize teaching us in Chicago. I fully immersed myself in Spanish to learn the language in a new environment and school. The most challenging part was right after we arrived on the Caribbean Island. Purely innocent at the age of ten. I used to wonder about women's clothing sometimes. I enjoyed the feel of satin lingerie and women's clothing style. Everything changed one afternoon, and I discovered a new world of sexuality at a young age.

The horror of being raped by my uncle at twelve changed everything, but despite the fear, this event helped me realize something unexpected - that I enjoyed the sexual experience. Surprisingly, amidst the trauma, the rape also helped me discover a new aspect of myself - my love for femininity and the attention I received from boys. With this newfound understanding, I started exploring cross-dressing. However, I wondered, what would be the next step? Unfortunately, my mom's clothing was too big for me.

My parents would often leave us home alone while they went to church. Having boys over for sexual encounters was exciting. However, one day, I got caught and things took a drastic turn. Unfortunately, my dad was not open-minded about it and his reaction was extremely abusive. As a result, my siblings and I endured years of unimaginable suffering, facing mental, verbal, physical, and sexual abuse from our father. We lived consumed by a constant state of fear.

I enjoyed engaging in sexual activities with boys, all the while embracing my preference for wearing lingerie. It became a weekly occurrence. To satisfy my desire to feel more feminine, I started taking underwear from clotheslines belonging to my cousins, sisters, and other girls in the neighborhood. I accumulated a collection of panties and other clothing items, which I stored in a shoe box in my room. One day, while I was away, my mother stumbled upon the box, which left her feeling saddened.

My mother was a dedicated Christian who instilled in her children the principles that defined her and influenced her own life. During my journey of grappling with my gender identity, she provided me with solace and support. In moments of despair, I shed tears, yearning for a different physical form, but it remained nothing more than a distant fantasy.

My mother was kind, but my father was challenging. Unfortunately, he constantly subjected me and my siblings to physical, verbal, and mental abuse. Being the second of six children, I often wished I were a girl just to avoid the constant abuse.

Despite his heavyset frame, my father moved with impressive agility during a fit of explosive anger. As I played in the front yard, he sharpened a new machete, his frustration growing. Suddenly, he got mad at me, shouting fiercely and brandishing a freshly sharpened weapon. Terrified, I sprinted away, sensing the approaching horror as he yelled that it was dull.

My childhood home was a small house in a mountain village near Dorado, close to the coast where you could hear the ocean at night and the Coqui singing at dawn. A peaceful and serene energy filled the air. We moved to a new community built by the people in the mid-'70s. It sat by the ocean, easily seen from a mile away, past a cow pasture.

Embracing change with new neighbors and schools. In my early teens, I started shaving my legs. No one noticed my dislike for my body hair because I was young. It took little effort. I wore girl's clothing, including short-cutout jeans, on days my parents were away.

The horror escalated and my dad became more abusive. The situation worsened, and I despised him. I missed the bus once and the librarian offered to drive me home. During the wait, I read books on cars, space, and technology.

The librarian drove me home, and my dad walked over with a fake smile, visibly angry. I entered the house and found myself in the living room. My dad's first action was to slap me upon entering. Exhausted and overwhelmed, I had reached my limit. He kept a machete ready by the door for the sugarcane field. I took advantage of this opportunity to release my teenage frustration and anger.

Before my dad could strike again, I grabbed the machete at the door and swung it at my dad, narrowly missing him. In fear, my mother screamed and confronted him about his abusive behavior.

I ran out of the house screaming after realizing I could have killed my dad. My mom hugged and cried upon catching up with me. My dad briefly slowed down, aware of potential trouble.

The police showed up at my parents' house and arrested my father. The reason, revealed days later, was that he had been raping my sisters. Mistreating children in Spanish countries can lead to vigilante justice.

The day signaled the end of his abuse, a man I despised. Thereafter, my mom moved back to our old home behind my grandparents.

I began a new life, liberated from my father's control, and able to be myself. My mom had a flexible Christian faith and loved her children. We now dwelled in a recently constructed house on the same property behind my grandparents' home. I can confidently claim my liberation and the freedom to do as I wish.

I felt free to be myself and transition as a woman. I felt sad, questioning my gender. I questioned the creator behind my mother's home late at night. The Coqui sang his enchanting melody as the wind blew through the mountains on a warm summer night.

I prayed, wondering why I was born male instead of female and why my wish to be a girl was not fulfilled. As morning came, I remained the same. I expressed my desire to God to turn into a girl overnight. The harsh reality of the situation was clear the next day. I dreamed of being a girl, longing to live as one.

I had the freedom to sleep and engage in sexual activities at my neighbor's home. He was my one and only boyfriend. In the outhouse behind my mom's home, I told him how I felt. I made my intentions for intimacy clear to him. I enjoyed drinking and sexual orgies, feeling like my authentic self and experiencing pure joy.

My free spirit ceased when I was jobless for a period, and job hunting in Puerto Rico was challenging then. My father spent little time in prison, he was a model prisoner and after leaving prison since my mom had divorced him after he left prison he moved to Atlanta, Georgia where he lived out the rest of his sentence after spending about five years in federal prison back in Puerto Rico.

After my father's imprisonment, my grandfather approached me and advised me I am now the man of the house and that I needed to quit school and go to work to help my mom support my siblings. I was thought to respect my elders and was close to grandfather; I loved him, this was sad since I loved school and had big dreams of being a scientist or an artist, I loved drawing but all that fell behind when I left school to work.

It was hard bouncing from one job to the next till I landed a job in Dorado painting murals with a Puerto Rican artist in the town. I worked there for six months till the job was completed and again bounced around from one job to another. I spent my free time going to bars when I was still too young, but no one ever questioned me.

I had sexual experiences with gay men, but it wasn't what I wanted until I encountered cross-dressers. I made friends, but unemployment was tough. When I found out my dad was in Atlanta, Georgia, he offered to help me get a job and I had to move in with him.

I found myself right back with a man that, though I hated, but I wanted to give him a chance since he was willing to help me. He appeared changed, kinder but still controlling. He spent my hard-earned money on his plans and used our money to buy appliances, furniture, and a car during tax time. I realized I needed to make my own plans with my money.

He planned to buy a car during tax season, using his money and mine. My plans didn't align with his. I bought a moped with my tax money to assert my independence, but he got angry and demanded I return it. I defied him, asserting my unwillingness to comply.

The past came right back as he jumped across his bed and wanted to physically abuse me, as soon as I saw his intentions I ran right out the door and jumped on my new moped and drove to my aunt's apartment.

I explained the situation to my aunt at her apartment. She didn't approve of his approach and reprimanded her brother because she was aware of his past abusive behavior. As a result, I lived with her for the next few years.

I had access to women's clothing once more, so I started collecting lingerie and wearing women's clothes again. I wore women's clothes when alone, such an exciting time.

My beginning in Atlanta was challenging. I had to relearn English and figure out how to navigate a foreign land. I bought my first car and got my driver's license, now I'm free to make my own decisions.

I moved in with a girlfriend after leaving my aunt's apartment, but it didn't work out because she found out about my love for women's clothing. We lived together but had separate sleeping arrangements. We lived together for three years, but I eventually moved out to live as a woman.

Living as a woman for six months, I craved a familiar setting with family due to the lack of internet and a supportive community. I moved back to my aunt's place and lived with her for the next couple of years or so, by then it was in the early '90s that I once more sought a new start in life with someone who really cares.

In mid-1992, a 5' Japanese woman stole my heart while I had a broken leg from a car accident. I told her about my gender issues, but she graciously brushed me off and changed my life. We lived for six months in the city of Marietta in a single-room apartment, and we got married in 1993.

In 1994, our first child, Katiya, was born in the city of Smyrna, Georgia. And in 1994 my son was born during the Atlanta Olympics. I tried to live as a man and care for my children and home, but I couldn't ignore the burning desire to become the woman I always dreamed of.

Here is a record from my initial therapy sessions after I came out. I shared this with my therapist during my first evaluation for gender dysphoria.

Difficult

Though this was supposed to be the most exciting time in anyone's life there was so much I had questioned in my mind and wanted so much to be a man to this woman I met and eventually married just nine months after we met.

Life was going well, we purchased our home in Powder Springs, Georgia in 1999 but something saddened me since despite how well all seemed to go, it was hard pretending to be a man that inside I know I am not I was not happy. Things began to change once more and though I tried to avoid it I would again start dressing in women's clothes, I began buying online.

The internet opened a new door I did not know existed till 1996 when I bought my first computer and almost immediately I began to research and read online about transgenders; I did not even know what the word meant till then and read and read so much about it and then began to read articles about men growing breast.

I thought that growing breasts was only something that naturally gendered females can grow, little did I know that men's breast tissue is the same as a woman's since it's mostly fatty tissue, no special muscles or anything else other than estrogen and progesterone. I learned that all babies are natural females, and it is only hormonal changes in the womb that trigger the change from female to male and so much I did not know before.

Challenging

My life has been full of challenges since childhood, but one of the biggest challenges I've faced is the discrepancy between my assigned gender at birth and my true identity as a woman. Despite being assigned male, I have always felt like a woman on the inside. Now, I am determined to let that woman out of this male body.

One aspect of my physical appearance that I have been struggling with is the hair on my body. Since it first grew, I have been shaving it, but none of the products I've tried have worked effectively. This has been frustrating, as I yearn to remove this hair and achieve a smoother, more feminine look.

Additionally, I have also experimented with various methods to enhance my breasts, longing for a more feminine silhouette. While I have experienced some limited success, my breasts feel as if they want to burst out of my chest. I have even noticed some flesh growth, which further emphasizes my desire for a well-shaped, woman's body.

In conclusion, I am determined to break free from the constraints of my current physical appearance and embrace a beautifully formed woman's body.

New Milestone at Sixty

A thank you note to my friends as I celebrate my sixtieth birthday. Thank you, my friends, for being here to celebrate my birthday. This is not only a celebration of my birthday but a celebration of a major milestone for me as Tamara Rivera. I am proud to be here with you celebrating such a joyous occasion. Without your support and friendship, I wouldn't be here.

The year 2021 was a hard, however, it was the year that ended on a high note and opened the door to a new journey in 2022. On October 10, 2021, I came out to the world and COX Automotive as transgender woman, your support and loyal friendship helped me take a bold step forward.

Today Tamara is proud of herself, strong, vibrant, powerful, full of potential, and has a future ahead with friends such as you I am possible.

A Difficult Choice

What's in a name?

Have you ever thought about this? Have you considered the meaning behind your name? Your name has a profound significance. The less common the name, the more unique it is. What if you had the chance to change your given name? Why change your name and what new name would you choose? Perhaps a name that you believe has a greater impact on your personality and better defines who you are. So many questions in such a short sentence.

Tamara is the name I chose, not my birth name. What motivates people to change their name? Artists change their name for various reasons, such as aligning with their stage persona or brand.

Who is Tamara and why did I choose that name? The name given to me at birth represented years of pain in my life. I despised the name and couldn't detach it from painful memories. I wanted to change the name for years, but I needed to research my options.

I would go online and find female names that represent beauty, passion, and have a greater impact on my personality. I had to find a defining name that reflects my gender and identity.

I used many names online in the past, but none defined me or had significance. My research continued for years trying to find the missing piece. Like a puzzle laid on a table for years to find the "missing piece" I am a transgender woman, and I wanted to know that when the time is right and I decide to change my name, there was no going back.

In mid-2021, I researched names with the letter T to find a name that wouldn't require changing my signature or much else. I found a list of 100 baby girl names starting with T. It's a big list to choose from for that one special name.

Tamara was the twentieth name in line. I paused briefly as I glanced at it. Reflecting on it, it seemed to be whispering, "Pick me," and so I opted for Tamara. However, before finalizing a name, it had to possess a profound meaning, stand out, and be truly one-of-a-kind.

My research led me to the discovery that Tamara, a name of Hebrew origin, means "palm tree" dating back 2000 centuries.

It is a Russian variant of the Biblical name Tamar "date or palm tree." This sweet moniker is symbolic of the beauty and fruitfulness associated with this tree. Until today, Tamara remains a popular name in Slavic languages. In the US, it was popular in the twentieth century, but now it's rather rare. It also means "spice" in Sanskrit *(an ancient Hindi language)*.

Once I was certain about living as a transgender woman and chose a name, I went to Cobb County Superior Court on November 20, 2021, to file for a legal name change.

They set the court date for Thursday, December 30, 2021, at 10:00 a.m. one day before the New Year. My nerves were on edge and I did not want to hear an objection. They conducted the session online, and I noticed the judge was a woman, not that it mattered.

Some people had divorce filings, the first two being such cases. I waited for my turn, expecting a long wait because of my last name, Rivera. To my surprise, I was called third while sitting in my office chair at home.

I wore a beautiful flowery top, makeup, and a nice pair of earrings, if I am changing my legal name to a female name, I wanted the judge to know that I mean business.

The judge asked if I truly wanted to change my first name from Tomas to Tamara. I responded, "yes, your honor." She asked if I was avoiding my creditors. I chuckled when she said, "Many people would do that." She looked at me, acknowledging my personal choice. I found that very meaningful. Despite the digital divide, she embraced my personal choice.

With a smile on her face, she said the last thing at the drop of the gavel, "From this day forth in the Cobb County Superior Court and the State of Georgia and by the powers vested in me, I now pronounce you Tamara Rivera."

I felt like floating on a cloud that day. I am a new person, liberated from a painful name. I wasted no time in announcing the news to the world, and 2022 became the beginning of my new journey.

In the past two years, I've experienced interesting life challenges such as anxiety and moving to a new place close to my children.

The first participation in the Atlanta PRIDE event on October 2022, hosted by Cox Automotive

United by Our Uniqueness

COMING OUT DAY interview questions

Interview each other in a way that feels comfortable for both of you. You might have a conversation about your experiences more than a formal interview.

    These questions are only suggestions:

Creative Questions

At what age did you realize you were gay?

Most people that question their sexuality begin at an early age, as it was for me. According to my research, I found that "Most people categorize their own gender on average between five and six years of age. In my case, my first encounter was at the age of five. Back then I knew there was something different as I questioned why I was born a boy when I did not feel like one.

When and how did you decide to come out?

I came out at the age of fifty-nine.

How did you come out and to whom?

I first decided to talk to COX as a transgender because I knew they were an LGBTQ+-friendly company. I wanted to make sure that my employer was there for me and for my family second.

Did you feel supported?

I really felt well supported by COX and my coworkers though some felt like they were not genuine, most did me and I felt very well accepted. With my family is a different story. Though my ex-wife and children accepted me as a transgender, my brother and most of my sisters rejected me and chose to never talk to me again.

What was the most positive reaction you received and what didn't go so well?

I had a Teams meeting in which COX introduced me as Tamara Rivera, that day there was some confusion as some were asked "Who is Tamara?" I saw the first message in the chatroom, everyone was surprised when they announced my coming out company-wide as Tamara and everyone congratulated me for my courage.

For the 2022 COX Inclusion and Diversity, I made a video that made it across the company from the East to the West Coast that same week I had employees from Georgia, Texas, and California reach out to me and some even stated that I inspired them to have more courage.

What did you wish you had at that moment to feel supported?

I wish I had made the announcement earlier on; I knew there were a few people here that were LGBTQ+ allies or were in the community themselves, but I held for so long suffering inside till that day I had the courage to speak up.

Did you grow up in a community that made coming out feel especially daunting?

(Community could be defined as your family, your church, your school, your town, etc.)

I grew up knowing that there was something different about me in a very religious family of Christian faith where there were men and women and nothing else.

Everyone else outside of that was an outcast, a reject or a negative side effect and the minute you deviate from the norm, there was pain and suffering. As I grew up, I really questioned my sexuality, I thought I was gay and though I had gay friends and I pretended to be, I knew that is not what I wanted, but I did not know who I was or what I was.

Growing up was very difficult and I got beat up many times by a father that thought he was going to make a man out of me by doing so. My life was miserable and many times late at night while everyone slept, I would go outside to the back of my parent's home in Puerto Rico and I would either lay face down on the ground or on my knees as I cried asked God, "Why did you make me a boy when I feel so much like a woman?"

What were your concerns, if any, about how coming out might affect you professionally?

I was always scared of what would happen if I came out as transgender, would I lose my job? What about my family? Would I lose it all? I walked the halls of the office looking at women, how beautiful they looked in the clothes and colors they wore, and imagined myself dressed as they dressed, but I always had that question in my head that made me so afraid of taking the step to come out: "What will happen if I lose my job?"

Have you ever dealt with discrimination or negative comments from coworkers or supervisors?

Some people may not agree with my move and though some have told me they don't agree with me, they accept me for who I am and honestly congratulated me. I never expected everyone to accept me, and I do appreciate the few people that were at least honest about it.

It's the ones that don't like it and don't speak up that I'm afraid of, but everyone has treated me with respect, not so much for coming out but because over the years I have earned that respect and some people actually did tell me that they knew or suspected I was different, but they never asked because they were also afraid to ask or offend me.

As for the managers and supervisors, I do feel there is a certain level of discomfort from some or that they publicly accepted me, but are not comfortable with me, but never would say anything out of respect, but I know that not everyone is going to be as accepting.

**Do you have any advice to share with someone
who is considering coming out?**

Today's society is very accepting of other gender roles and social media makes it easier for people to express their gender identity. However, there is still a lot of fear, which I am aware of. Suicide is usually what some would consider as a way out.

Whenever I have the opportunity to encourage someone, I let them know there is a lot of help out there and a lot of resources to help them, I am a member of the Human Rights Campaign (HRC) and other organizations that I know of and I have a few transgender friends on Facebook and if someone asks for advice, I freely and warmly give advice to anyone to not be afraid. I encourage anyone to come out as early as you can, so you don't have to suffer through life as much as I have.

**Why did you decide to speak out in honor
of National Coming Out Day?**

National Coming Out Day was like an open door for me to learn more about the LGBTQ+ community and resources. I am more involved today than I was before since I am no longer afraid. I wanted to speak out and would love to speak out in other engagements because I believe that my story can really inspire others in a positive way.

In your mind, why is National Coming Out Day important?

This is very important, though socially we have grown so much, politically there are a lot of barriers against the LGBTQ+ community based on standard, religious, and social stigma. When I was growing up and still today, a lot of people have a negative outlook f transgender people.

They are more accepting of gays and lesbians but when it relates to the transgender community there is so much need for education.

What are authentic ways corporations can support employees exist openly?

I am aware that there are large corporations out there that are LGBTQ+ inclusive such as COX, Google, Amazon, and others, but when it comes to smaller employers or mom-and-pop stores that don't want to accept it and will not hire LGBTQ+ people, employers of all sizes need to be educated and trained on how to hire and employ transgender people, we are people of many talents and backgrounds and bring a lot to the table to make any company a successful business. We need to educate more companies on the benefits that the LGBTQ+ community brings to their doorsteps.

What is the biggest lesson you learned in this process of finding yourself?

I wish I had started earlier in life. However, I also feel that there was a bigger reason in my life for coming out at the right moment in my life. Today I have more female friends on Facebook, at least 80 percent or more of my audience is cisgender and transgender women whom I communicate with and positively encourage to be strong and to stand on their own.

Also since 2022 rolled in I worked hard to build myself up, lose weight and improve my health, since January I have been working towards my goal, exercising every morning and walking twice a day, I went from 195lbs to 155 lbs. where I am today and I am also inspiring other women in my neighborhood to walk and I am trying to work to create a neighborhood walk club. I have had several women tell me that I have inspired them and that means a lot to me.

Who has been your biggest supporter through it all?

My biggest supporters are some of my newest female friends and some of my longtime friends. I did lose family and friends, but I learned that the friends I lost were never my friends. I have a few close cisgender female friends that I talk to daily.

How would you describe the experience of being out as an employee of Cox?

The overall experience has been very positive. Anyone I talk to about COX has been in a very positive manner since COX has been there for me. I have many friends that work for this company, some whom I know closely and some from far away from the East to the West Coast.

There are many COX Automotive employees that know me since I began working for this company in 2008, many of these employees know that I'm very savvy with technology and they know that if Tamara can't help them, more likely, no one can. They know that if I don't have an answer, I'll find it or at least provide them with other resources, I even have employees that refer others to me because they know and trust that I am going to do my best to help them, and it gives me more confidence and reasons to love my work.

My First Contest as a Transgender Woman

My FabOver40 contest statement

I am a transgender woman breaking the barriers and boundaries others say I couldn't touch, competing where competition is fierce, I am the first transgender woman competing in the FabOver40 contest to receive a two-page spread in *Newbeauty* magazine, $40,000 cash, and a spa-cation! To benefit the National Breast Cancer Foundation INC.

Please join me in the fight for the cure. I lost my mother thirty-five years ago to breast cancer at forty-seven. She was young, vibrant, and energetic, carrying a big smile and a loving heart to everyone whose life she touched. This means a lot to me, and I would love your vote, please go to https://votefab40.com/2022/tamara-rivera and cast your vote for Tamara Rivera, only you can decide if I am FabOver40.

This contest was engaging, and I was the first transgender woman to take part. I had a chance of winning, and I emerged victorious in the first phase but regrettably couldn't clinch the prize in the second phase of the contest as it grew more competitive. Though I did not win, I am a winner as the first time a transgender woman to take part in this contest.

My Daily Diary to Transition into Tamara Rivera.

2021/05/10 Hormones Weekly Log

After so much delay, I decided to finally seek an LGBT specialist and get the counseling and medical care I needed, and after weeks of tests and medical evaluations, I finally was approved to start my hormones. I was prescribed Estradiol, which are female hormones, as well as Spironolactone, a testosterone blocker. I started taking them on the same day, marking the beginning of my new journey.

2021/05/15 - Today is my fifth day since I started taking hormone replacement therapy (HRT), and I can't help but notice the subtle changes in my body. As I gently touch my chest, I feel a slight fullness in my breasts, as if they are blossoming into something new. Last night, as I measured them, I couldn't help but smile as I realized they had grown about an inch since the last time.

2021/05/16 - Every day I keep monitoring myself to see if there are any changes in my body, hoping to see more breast tissue and more hip and butt. Changes such as this take time. I'm just hoping it's faster. This afternoon after painting my porch and spending some time outside, I came back inside from the searing heat. I took some time to remove my clear nail enamel and clean them and after taking a shower I manicured my nails and sat for a bit while watching TV and I felt my breasts, like, almost breaking out of my shirt, feeling full and firm.

2021/05/17 I have this strange sensation that my breasts are expanding, almost as if they are bursting out of my chest. However, apart from this peculiar feeling, I haven't noticed any other changes yet. I received a notification today about a package delivery from Wholesale7. The package was supposed to contain orange platform shoes and an orange dress. Unfortunately, to my disappointment, the package never arrived.

2021/05/18 - I just woke up and got my day started. The first thing on my agenda is my daily stretching exercises. After that, I take my dose of hormones. Once I've had breakfast, it's time for me to start working at my home office.

2021/05/19 - I'm feeling a bit sleepy this morning. I'm just getting started and after my morning exercise routine and a fresh cup of coffee, I felt better. Later while working from home, I watched a movie that made me laugh and cry, in the end, it was marked as the best cross-dresser movie ever and titled Just Like a Woman. It was good, and I cried because I could see myself in the same dilemma as the male cross-dresser in the movie and wished my life had as happy an ending as he had.

2021/05/20 - Today I had a busy day, got up early and headed out the door with my brother to Chattanooga, Tennessee to pick up a truck to bring back to Atlanta. We had a delay, but we got back by 3:30 p.m. After dropping off the truck at his home, he brought me back home and I realized that I left my keys inside his truck so with his help I broke into my own home by breaking the lock on the garage door to get in and later I had to buy a new lock to replace the one I broke.

2021/05/21 - I was feeling sleepy after being abruptly awakened by a loud crashing sound. Consequently, I couldn't sleep much afterwards. Additionally, this morning I took the opportunity to measure my chest, only to discover that it measured half an inch more than the last time I checked.

2021/05/22 - Today is twelve days since I started HRT, I'm not yet noticing considerable progress, every day my breasts do feel full but occasionally feel a bit less so this may be normal breast changes.

2021/05/23 - Today I woke up feeling rested and ready for the day. I did my morning exercise routine and took my hormones. While having breakfast, I could feel my breasts full and as I massaged my breasts it felt firm.

2021/05/24 - I had a good day today, I got up at the usual time, did my morning exercise routine, and had a smooth day working from home. After getting off work, I mowed the lawn and cooked dinner. I am ready for bed after my usual exercise routine before bed.

2021/05/25 - I woke up a bit sleepy today and had less energy than usual so I took a nap during my lunch break and at the end of the day nightfall I went to sleep thirty minutes early.

2021/05/26 - I woke up this morning feeling rested and energized, and I worked out a bit longer than usual. Working out daily has been an obsession and some days I want to set limits while other days I go the extra mile to hit a higher goal than the day before and it feels great.

2021/05/27 - After a restful night's sleep, I'm feeling refreshed and ready to start the day. However, I've noticed that my breast doesn't feel as full as they have been in the past few days. I believe this fluctuation is normal, as breast size can vary over time. To enhance breast growth, I've placed an order for Pueraria breast cream, which is expected to arrive tomorrow.

2021/05/28 - Today I woke up feeling great. After taking my hormones and getting in some exercise, I am fully prepared for the day ahead. It's been a while since I last felt my breasts feeling full, but now, as I sit in my living room and enjoy a movie, that sensation has returned while I unwind. Before long, I'll be winding down for bed.

2021/05/29 - Last night I had trouble sleeping and after sitting up in bed twice, at last, I was able to sleep around 1:30 a.m. and woke up this morning around 5:45 a.m. so I still have not gotten much sleep and didn't have much energy to exercise this morning. Tomorrow is my birthday and twenty days since I began HRT, though I have not seen much progress, I'm sure time will tell.

2021/05/30 - Today I woke up and felt happy in my breast once again feeling like it's busting out of my chest, today is my fifty-ninth birthday and this comes as a gift. I have been thinking about moving away from home for a while to either sunny Florida to be close to NASA or the Longhorn state of Texas close to Boca Chica to be close to the SpaceX Starship facility and the home of Starbase, Texas. I have looked at many rental properties or the possibility of buying a low-price mobile home.

2021/05/31 - Today I woke up feeling sleepy and did not have much energy to exercise, but I'm going for it. The last day of May today is Labor Day weekend and I'm looking forward to a cookout on a cool day.

2021/06/01 - Today I woke up wondering how long it will be before I can see significant improvement from taking HRT. There are times when I feel the changes in my body and moments when I feel like nothing is going on. Just nine days more for my one month on hormones, what are the next thirty days going to be like?

2021/06/02 - I got up today feeling rested and ready for the day. After my morning exercise routine and breakfast, I was ready for work and had a smooth day. Today after a four-day delay I got my breast cream and am ready to start tonight with breast massage twice a day and see how much better the results are in a month.

2021/06/03 - Got up early this morning feeling good and looking forward to a good day. Lately, for the past week, I noticed that my blood pressure is lower on average just below normal.

2021/06/04 - Today I got up and did my usual exercise routine and took a shower. After that, I did my nails and dressed for work as usual in women's clothing. While working my mind was wondering and during lunch, I broke down into tears, I'm planning on coming out to my employer and looking for all the help I can get to make my transition a reality, but so many things are going through my mind that I broke down in tears. I think the stress earlier today brought my blood pressure up to 140 but after a bit of stretching and releasing shoulder tension, I felt better.

2021/06/05 - I slept well last night and woke up early this morning, got up and did my usual exercise routine, trimmed my toenails, and shaved. After some self TLC. I had a bowl of cereal and coffee.

2021/06/06 - Today I woke up with not much desire to do my daily exercises, I got up and stretched for a couple of minutes and then proceeded to my schedule of daily exercise routine some days I just have to push myself to just do it.

2021/06/07 - I got up this morning with so much going through my mind, I'm ready to tell my family about moving from home but so many worries are going through my mind, how is my family going to take this? For now, I can only hope that it all goes well. I'm thinking of moving to Texas but what are the state's rules for LGBT groups? I noticed today that my left hand was hurting from arthritis pain and I'm hardly able to close my fist or put pressure on my hand. I was able to do my morning exercise routine, though.

2021/06/08 - After a good night's sleep, I woke up feeling refreshed and ready for the day ahead. However, I couldn't ignore the persistent pain in my left hand that had been bothering me for the past two days due to arthritis. Thankfully, I can now say that I'm feeling much better.

2021/06/09 - This morning I got up a bit later than usual, but I'm ready for the day. OMG, I'm very tired today after work, I guess it was more boring than other times. I am seriously considering having a talk with HR to open up to my company as M2F in transition so this can open up the conversation and help my progress.

2021/06/10 - Today is my anniversary, thirty days since I started my HRT, and I am wondering when will I be able to see signs of changes in my body. I often feel my breasts full and though they have not grown much, it feels like it's growing wider, and I can feel the difference from thirty days ago. What would the next thirty days be like?

2021/06/11 - Today is another step in my transition to M2F a new month to my future self to life as a female, it feels like every day is a new beginning of discovery. Today almost all day my breast felt full and a bit soar like when your muscles feel after you exercise. Could this be the progress of a growing breast?

2021/06/12 - I got out of bed later than usual and did not have time for my usual exercise routine. After waking, I had breakfast and left. I planned to go to Brands Mart to buy a new radio for my 2012 Hyundai Veloster. The radio wasn't expensive, but the installation was not within my budget.

Later I went to Best Buy but they did not have any radios for my car, by this time I drove much around, disappointed I returned home and went to the auto parts store to get refrigerant for my car since the air conditioner was not cooling, and since I've never done this before I went on to YouTube to see videos on how it's done.

After learning how to do this and following the steps on my car, another disappointment set on after realizing that after almost filling up the system with refrigerant, the air was still not cool and the pressure started dropping, that led to only one conclusion, a system leak. I spent a lot of time running around town and ended up disappointed, but my younger sister visited me in the end.

2021/06/13 - I had a good start today, after I got up and did my usual exercise routine and had breakfast with my daughter, I sat in the living room for a while and then went shopping I went to Burger King and returned home, and my son finally got the air conditioner on my car working and now it cools well.

2021/06/14 - I just woke up and am getting started for the day. Today is the day I will iron my hair for the very first time, something I've always wanted to do. It's the end of the day, no iron for hair, but tomorrow is another day.

2021/06/15 The Hair I Always Wanted

I woke up feeling good and eager to try my new flat hair iron. I successfully styled my hair for the first time at lunch, but I struggled with the sides and burned myself. I'm going to a professional stylist do my hair.

2021/06/16 - Unexpected Shopping Day

A good night's sleep left me refreshed and ready. I had to return an Amazon package to Kohl's after work. I received a 25% off coupon for in-store purchases. While leaving, I noticed a hot comb that I bought. It worked better than my flat iron, and now my hair is soft and ready to be styled.

2021/06/17 - Staying up late

Stay up late and pay the price in the morning. I stayed up later than usual till midnight and I'm feeling sleepy this morning… oh well! I got up and checked the mirror. Last night, I felt disappointed after I straightened my curly hair, took a shower, and saw that it went back to being curly. This morning, I straightened my hair and I'm avoiding water for a few days.

2021/06/18 - Transgender Struggles

I woke up this morning feeling sleepy, and after my usual exercise routine, I felt better and ready for today's challenges. Every day as a transgender woman, I have a new beginning to explore the possibilities and gain acceptance from my friends and family, which in most cases feels like climbing a mountain.

2021/06/19 - The Stranger in the Dark

I had the strangest dream last night, I was in a large open room like an open meeting room but filled with beds of sleeping souls and it was dark and a sliver of light down an open walkway down the middle of the room,

I sought someone in the dimly lit middle of the hallway, but didn't want to wake everyone by turning on the light. In the hallway, I felt a presence but couldn't see anything, just a shadow. I felt a large hairy hand in front of my face, then woke up scared and sweating.

2021/06/20 Father's Day

Today I woke up late so when I got out of bed and realized that today was Father's Day, I knew that both my children will be home since my daughter's birthday is on Tuesday we made it a double event since she may not be here on that day. Despite the cloudy day, we had fun. My son made dinner and later we celebrated my daughter's birthday.

2021/06/21 Feeling Overwhelmed

I woke up feeling good today, but things went downhill before lunch. A coworker annoyed me with small, unimportant issues that they were blowing out of proportion. I chose to ignore his private messages, but he called me and I confronted him. I had little interest in interacting with others due to my illness and lack of energy.

I felt an overwhelming sadness and had the urge to cry without cause. When he called me, I felt like someone had just struck a match and I flared up like a stove when you open the gas valve to light it up and hung up on him. He called me three times, and I ignored him and then he began sending me multiple messages, which I also ignored. I took a nap during lunch and felt a bit better, but that event made my day hard and tiring.

2021/06/22 Early Riser

This morning I got up an hour early and sat in bed playing solitaire on my phone and thirty minutes later, I got out of bed and did my daily exercise routine, right at 7:00 a.m. I headed to the kitchen for breakfast.

2021/06/23 Burning Sensation

I had a restful sleep last night, but this morning I woke up with a burning sensation in my left eye, as if it had been scratched. I quickly got out of bed and examined my reflection in the mirror, only to find that my eye appeared bloodshot. To alleviate the discomfort, I proceeded to cleanse my face with cold water, resulting in some relief.

I'm getting ready for my usual exercise routine and ready for the day.

I have been ironing out my curly hair for a few days since getting a hot hairbrush and I like the results so I'm playing with it to get better, but I know I need a haircut since I have not seen a barber in about three months.

It's been close to sixty days since I started taking HRT and aside from feeling like my breast is busting out of my chest, I have seen little progress.

2021/06/24 Late Riser

Today I woke up a bit later than usual and still sat in bed with my head down. I took a quick nap and then got up. I start my mornings by monitoring my blood pressure, taking hormones, and exercising for at least 10 minutes.

2021/06/25 Smooth Day

Today started like any other day. I woke up as usual and went about my routine tasks. The day went by smoothly, without any major hiccups. As the day ended, I found myself going to bed later than usual. But that's alright, because tomorrow is a new day.

2021/06/26 Sunny Day

Today woke up late since I went to sleep late last night, was still sleepy, but I had work to do. First on my agenda was yard work to clean up the front and backyard and later I was going to get a cute haircut. My day was busy, and I couldn't find time for a haircut. I'm going to bed early to catch up on lost sleep.

2021/06/27 The Long Overdue Haircut

Today is the day for my long-awaited haircut. It's been three months and my hair has grown so much. Opted for a unisex style, can't wait to see the result.

Later today I'm going to a funeral to see a tragically departed second cousin twenty-eight years old of a heart attack, so young and so much potential cut short.

Finally, I got my hair done and later drove to the funeral and saw family members I had not seen in a while. We had dinner after the funeral, and when I got home, I fell asleep on the couch because of exhaustion.

2021/06/29 Feeling Better

Despite having a tension headache before bedtime, I still managed to sleep well and woke up feeling refreshed. The start of the night was rather uneventful, with not much happening.

2021/06/30 My Day Off

Today I took the day off to unwind and though it started off as usual after my daily exercise routine and breakfast is when it all started. After a bowl of cereal and coffee, I went to the backyard to blow out the dry grass from last Sunday's lawn mower clippings, and that only took thirty minutes.

I spent at least three hours cleaning and organizing the garage. Yard work, along with other tasks, occupied most of the day due to the humid weather and lunchtime nearing. I was exhausted and slept on the couch for nearly an hour after lunch. I felt much better after showering.

At the end of the day, I did my hair with my hot hairbrush, I'm getting better at it, also as time goes by, I can't ignore my breast which measured a bit more than the last time I checked a month ago so now I'm up to 43 ½ inches.

2021/07/01 A Working Radio

Today, my car radio from eBay finally arrived after a delay. After work, I planned to install and test the radio on my 2012 Hyundai Veloster. All tests passed, and the radio worked flawlessly after setup and pairing it with my phone.

2021/07/02 Hard Rise

I struggled to get out of bed this morning. I had a long nap yesterday and struggled to sleep at night, resulting in fatigue this morning. HRT has led to smoother skin, reduced body hair, and improved blood pressure.

2021/07/03 My Morning Routine

Waking up refreshed is good for facing today's challenges. I played my usual game of Microsoft Solitaire after getting out of bed. Each morning, I listen to Google News while playing solitaire. First, I check my blood pressure and take my hormones, then I do my exercise routine and make the bed. It's now my morning routine.

2021/07/04 What a Good Morning!

I woke up refreshed and ready for the Fourth of July. The Fourth of July came and went out with fireworks display at my sister's house in a cul-de-sac. The air was calm and warm, and we had the best display at the time. All neighbors were impressed by the fireworks as they rose high in the air, creating colorful streams of sound and light in the sky. We all had fun.

2021/07/05 The Fifth Day

Today, I had a late start and lacked motivation. Nevertheless, I made pancakes for breakfast. Unexpectedly, I ended up having a hectic day. Now, I'm looking forward to getting some rest before going back to work tomorrow.

2021/07/06 I Slept Like a Log

I sleep like a log undisturbed. Why, you may wonder? Logs don't sleep. I slept well and woke up at 5:30 a.m. without interruption. I checked my blood pressure, which was 104/72, did my morning exercise, and got ready for the day.

I've had two consecutive playback wins, could I be close to winning the lottery?

I've noticed tenderness and growth around my nipples, possibly indicating more breast tissue growth.

2021/07/07 Busy Morning

I got up this morning feeling energetic. I have been massaging my breasts twice a day for the past month to promote growth and increase blood flow. My breasts have increased by half an inch since last month.

2021/07/08 Nothing but the Usual

I started my day as usual: checking my blood pressure, doing my exercises, getting dressed, having breakfast, and heading to my home office to work. I have enjoyed working from home for almost two years since COVID-19.

2021/07/10 Pandemic Woes

I have no plans or idea on what to do or where to go due to the pandemic and people's fear of infection.

Today is my 60th day of taking HRT and I've noticed minor changes like wider hips and bigger breasts. How will the next thirty days before my next appointment with my doctor unfold?

2021/07/11 Day For Relaxation

Today I woke up earlier than usual and after my morning routine, I felt relaxed and refreshed. After breakfast, I relaxed in the kitchen, reading the news and going through my emails while enjoying the fresh air from the open window.

I spent some time cleaning my car inside and since I washed it the day before, and I took the time to wax and detail my car, I've always liked a clean car and it makes me feel good to clean every crevice as much as possible.

2021/07/12 Laundry Day

Today was one of those days when you realize you need to organize your clothes and do your laundry. I did laundry while working and organized clothes at lunch. Work consumed my day, leaving little time for other activities.

2021/07/14 I Need More Sleep

Today was a great day. I talked to my manager about coming out as a transgender woman. Opening up to her brought relief, and I may share more later.

For the last two weeks, I've noticed that even though I'm going to bed at the usual time, 11:00 p.m. Is my sleepiness caused by lack of sleep or poor-quality of sleep? No matter what, I'll try going to bed one hour earlier.

2021/07/15 Ready For Today

I have an early virtual meeting with a new therapist today, sponsored by my company for up to eight free sessions. The first virtual session with my new therapist was disrupted by network issues, so we ended up talking on the phone. We can learn from each other since I'm her first transgender client. It will be an interesting experience.

2021/07/17 Too Early

I'm an early riser, usually waking up at 5:30 a.m. This is my daily schedule seven days a week. It may seem early, but I've been doing this for a while.

Upon waking up, I am usually energized enough for my exercise routine. I prioritize exercise and my health routine before beginning my day, even on days when I lack motivation.

2021/07/18 Rise-n-Shine

I woke up to the soft rays of the morning sun peering through my curtains, casting a warm golden glow on my bedroom walls. The gentle chirping of birds outside filled the air, creating a soothing symphony of nature's melodies. As I went through my morning routine, the invigorating scent of freshly brewed coffee wafted from the kitchen, awakening my senses. With no concrete plans in sight, I embraced the freedom of the day, ready to embark on an adventure of spontaneity.

2021/07/19 Changes Are Inevitable

Since starting HRT, I have noticed some significant changes, particularly in how it affects my mood, thoughts, and feelings. As a result, I have been inspired to make some adjustments in my life, such as changing my hairstyle and placing a greater emphasis on self-care.

2021/07/20 Good Start-Bad Day

My day started normal, then went downhill. I requested time off work due to feeling down, but my request was denied.

They declined my request for a five-day vacation, leaving me frustrated and angry. Despite calming down later, my plans were still ruined.

2021/07/22 Early Disappointment

Last night, I decided to start my day early, all prepared and dressed up. I thought about it, but then this morning I noticed my wife didn't get out of bed on time. She usually leaves the house at 6:00 a.m., but today she's leaving at 8:00 a.m. I had to reschedule my plan to get dolled up.

More disappointed with work, I've been getting denied every time I ask for time off. I requested two days this week and they denied it. I requested a vacation next week, and they only approved one day. When I requested vacation for the following week, they only approved four days. I'm feeling frustrated and neglected.

2021/07/23 Friday I'm Happy You Came

Is there anything else that requires an explanation? These past few days have been difficult, I'm happy it's Friday. The weekend is here and I'm looking forward to a better outcome next Monday.

I have been feeling stressed and getting fast heartbeats the past few days and for two days my blood pressure was a bit higher than it has been for the past six weeks.

It went up from an average of 118 to 125 due to a few stressful days. Today I decided to request FMLA to take some deserved time off to get my stress under control.

2021/07/24 Take My Time

I am progressively getting more into daily habits such as taking more time for self. I used facial soap, moisturizer, cream, and setting powder for the first time today, and my face felt amazing.

Also, before bed, I took the time to wash my face and add vitamin C serum. This will become my daily ritual. Since I began ironing out my hair, I have become more conscious and spending more time taking care of my hair. Gradually, I've been dedicating more time to self-care and prioritizing the little things that matter to me as a woman.

2021/07/25 Sick Day

I had a productive morning today. I got out of bed, took my hormones, exercised, and made a delicious breakfast of bagels with turkey bacon, eggs, and cheese with a cup of coffee. After breakfast, as I sat in the kitchen reading today's headlines, I felt a dose of flu with a runny nose and a light headache.

Despite my first thoughts of COVID, I set my fears aside and realized it may be allergies from cutting the grass the day before. I feelt better at bedtime after taking four thirty-minute naps today.

2021/07/26 A New Day, A New Outlook

To address my stress management needs, I sought FMLA. After calling my doctor's office, I have scheduled an appointment for tomorrow to discuss the possibility of taking extended leave for the sake of my mental well-being.

2021/07/27 What's Beyond the Horizon?

Like an explorer, I'm headed to my doctor's office, curious about what awaits.

I've noticed mood swings and other changes since starting HRT for my M2F transition. I have experienced a decrease in libido and erectile function for the past few months. My breasts feel constantly full and have increased in size by at least 1.5 inches.

Due to my mistake in reading the time, I arrived late to my doctor's appointment. I couldn't check in from the app because the scheduled time was no longer available, which seemed like a mistake. I found out the time was earlier and got rescheduled for Thursday.

2021/07/28 Up Early

My brain is overwhelmed with thoughts. I slept well last night and woke up at 5:00 this morning. I relieved my bladder and returned to bed. I played solitaire in bed until 6:00 a.m. after failing to go back to sleep.

I felt the need to write in my diary because my mind was overwhelmed. There are days when I lack inspiration and ideas for writing.

My blood pressure monitor displayed 147/80 last night, which surprised me since it has been normal for months. Three additional readings, but still not much improvement at 155/75.

With a bit of fear, I checked my blood pressure this morning, and it read on the monitor's display a perfect 120/80

2021/07/29 Second Time Around

My typical daily routine involves hormone intake, blood pressure check, and thirty minutes of exercise. My doctor's appointment was at 2:45 p.m. I finished work at 12:45 today.

I rushed to apply minimal makeup before leaving for my appointment. I encountered heavy traffic on I-20 while driving to my doctor's office, but I arrived on time. There was only one available parking spot upon arrival, which I thought was ideal.

After a quick twenty-minute visit to the doctor's office, I witnessed an awful sight. Discovering that my car had been booted, with a note providing a phone number and QR code for payment filled me with horror and anger. I paid $75 to remove the boot and waited in silence for 15 minutes.

2021/07/30 What a good feeling!

I went to bed 30 minutes earlier and woke up at 4:00 a.m. I went to the bathroom, returned to bed, and slept until 5:30 a.m. While in bed, I played solitaire on my phone and planned my day.

I finished my game at 5:55 a.m. and my blood pressure was 105/73. I woke up feeling positive and ready to start the day.

Tomorrow is the last day of July, marking my first 90 days on HRT. My breasts feel full daily and grow half an inch monthly, despite the minor changes. I am eager to see what lies ahead in the next ninety days.

2021/07/31 A Busy Day

I usually start my mornings with hormones, exercise, and a facial, but today I had important housework to do, so I went to Home Depot to replace the back door.

I wore a women's black t-shirt with a flower print and women's black yoga pants and a phone wallet where I had my driver's license and credit cards.

I walked to the back door display, selected two models, and then headed to a desk in the doors and windows department. Ralph at the desk provided help in acquiring the door shims, installation hardware, molding, and nails.

After all that, he also sat down and went online to show me a video of the installation process. Later I had to wait for a truck from the rental department and they as well were helpful.

After loading the door into a large rental van, I drove home and offloaded the door and headed back to Home Depot to return the van. I went back into the Home Depot and waited a while before installing the door, since the lock I purchased needed to be re-keyed.

Bobby, the locksmith, wasn't there, so I returned after lunch and had him re-key the lock. To install the door, I removed the old one, cleaned the area, and installed the new lock.

2021/08/01 I'm Gald it's Over.

Today, after getting dressed and ready, it was as busy as the previous day. I completed steps on the back door and installed a security sensor.

I spent a few hours helping my son clean the garage. After four hours of work, I felt sore from yesterday and today, but I'm glad it's over.

2021/08/02 I have No Words

Writing is unpredictable - sometimes I lack ideas, other times I have an overflow of thoughts. I hadn't written a diary before, but I could have filled container ships with books if I had started earlier.

I started writing when I began HRT for gender reassignment, never being so dedicated before. I now diligently prioritize self-care, exercise, and writing.

This has truly brought positive changes to my life. Caring for my hair involves regular maintenance and attending to my appearance, including painting my nails with a custom light pink shade.

I'm getting better at nail art. I am now giving my face the attention it deserves. Taking care of my appearance and health has been rewarding.

2021/08/03 More Time to Play

With my wife back to her school schedule, I have more time to indulge in makeup, clothing, and nail care. I've been practicing my nail art skills for months, improving with each attempt. YouTube and Instagram have been invaluable in learning from professionals.

I bought a package of Splat Rebellious Colors crimson red and am excited to see how it looks on my hair.

2021/08/04 What's Up Today?

Daily, I ponder my next steps, experimenting with new ideas and techniques to achieve my desired identity as a woman.

I watch YouTube videos daily about makeup, dressing up, and passing out as a woman; it's been my dream since childhood.

My breast size appears to be slowly increasing. I take prescribed hormones twice daily, including Spironolactone to block testosterone and Estradiol to change my body.

2021/08/05 Not A Good Day

It was a typical start to the day. I felt emotional and physically unwell, so I decided to take the rest of the day off work.

I felt slightly better in the afternoon, but my heart rate increased later in the day. My blood pressure dropped from 134/76 to 113/79 in 20 minutes.

During my time off today, I got new red nail polish, polish remover, and round cosmetic pads.

I successfully applied a hair relaxer kit for the second time, leaving my hair silky smooth.

I'm pleased with the results and even received a compliment from my wife, who said it looks better than when I used a hot comb. I was concerned about hair damage from using a hot comb.

2021/08/06 What's Happening?

I left work at 12:00 p.m. yesterday because of illness and called off today. My blood pressure has been good for the past two months, but the past two days it's been higher than usual.

2021/08/07 Reboot Time

Next week marks my three-month HRT anniversary, and I'm eager about my first follow-up with the doctor.

Your body can sense when something's wrong, as the past two days have shown. I was worried about a potential heart attack due to increased heart rate, tension in my neck and shoulders, and elevated blood pressure.

Last night, I skipped my usual exercises and spent 30 minutes in bed listening to meditation music. I performed my usual nightly routine, including hygiene and hormone intake. I dozed off while the music was playing.

I use my Google bedside speaker to play instrumental music as I fall asleep for 20 minutes. It reduces stress and improves my energy levels upon waking.

2021/08/08 Not Much to Say

Today was smooth. I've been exercising at a slower pace for the past two days due to feeling odd. I've been doing half sets to avoid pushing myself too hard. I took it easy all day.

I washed and waxed my car, went for a short drive, and returned home after 40 minutes. My son ordered Chinese food yesterday, so I had leftovers for dinner at 6:00 p.m.

After dinner, I watched the animated movie VIVO (Alive) on Netflix. It had a few emotional moments. I had an enjoyable time watching the movie.

2021/08/09 Four Days Is Better Than Nothing

This week, I'll take the four approved days off. I finally got a four-day vacation approved after multiple rejections.

My three-month follow-up appointment for HRT is on Wednesday. I've noticed breast tissue growth, wider hips, and smoother skin.

I have noticed changes in my personality, mood, and sensitivity, making me more prone to crying. I have paid more attention to my personal grooming, including my hair, appearance, and weight. What lies ahead in the next three months?

2021/08/10 Anticipation

Today I woke up earlier than usual, at 4:45 a.m. I was already awake and couldn't sleep much after that, I sat up in bed and played solitaire for a few minutes, and by 5:30 I asked my Google speaker to play out the news while I exercise and prepare myself for the day.

After running errands in the morning, I bought printer ink and visited a cosmetics store for the first time. I found a nearby Ulta Beauty in Lithia Springs, a few miles from my location.

The store was the biggest cosmetics store I've seen, with an overwhelming variety of products. During my brief visit, I purchased two nail polishes (green and clear), and a suggested concealer for my skin tone.

Despite overspending by $69, I viewed it as progress in my transition. I am eager to go to my doctor's office tomorrow.

2021/08/11 Happy Anniversary

I just hit my ninety-day mark on HRT for body feminization. Now waiting for blood work results to track changes.

The doctor will analyze today's blood work to potentially increase my estradiol dose and enhance my transition.

I prepared last night by doing my toenails and setting aside my clothes. I felt successful in my green outfit this morning and received compliments from the nurses, doctor, and receptionist.

Green is my best color, but I need to conquer makeup and fear of going out in public. It's embarrassing, but the fear is real.

One day after leaving my doctor's office, I felt I needed to pee, but since I was already out the door, I thought that I could not wait till I get home, which was a mistake.

While heading home, the urge became unbearable, and I couldn't wait any longer. Since I'm not passable and would have looked terrible using a men's restroom, I couldn't stop anywhere dressed as a woman.

My bladder burst five miles from home, forcing me to drive while urinating in my car. I had to shower and clean my car after arriving home soaked. I need to do my makeup to boost my confidence and overcome fear.

2021/08/12 More Details Later

Feeling more energized today, I exercised and did my morning routine. My only task for today is to go to Tires Plus and fix a broken wheel pressure sensor in my car.

I set up an appointment with a new therapist today who might be a good fit for me since he is gay and may be more understanding of my transgender identity. I'm waiting early for my appointment this Sunday at 1:00 p.m.

My blood test results were positive. I grew ½" in breast tissue per month, eager for the next three months.

2021/08/13 Last Day to Unwind

I took a few days off work to relax and rejuvenate. It's been 4 days and I'm in my living room with an open window. The wind is blowing a calm, chilly breeze as I take a deep breath. I am calm and refreshed, so it's been a successful time to relax and enjoy. Contemplating my transition, I am eager to embrace being a trans woman.

Occasionally, I feel like I'm drowning and all I can do is cry. Hormones or personal struggle, I can't tell. At times like these, I feel confused not knowing how to proceed in my transition.

I invest time in my appearance, envisioning a world where I am my authentic self and embraced. Happiness eludes me, though I deserve it.

2021/08/15 A Fresh Start

I woke up at 4:30 a.m. and dozed off at 5:30 a.m. I played solitaire in bed, checked my blood pressure, and did my morning exercise routine. I left my room and had fish for breakfast for the first time, which was satisfying and healthier.

This afternoon at 1:00 pm. I have a virtual meeting with a new therapist who speaks English and Spanish and is gay. I hope we can establish a good relationship.

I had a positive experience with my new therapist, Dr. Loriot. He is genuinely understanding and respectful. He even used my chosen gender name and pronoun, which made me feel comfortable.

2021/08/16 I have no Clue.

Some days you wake up feeling refreshed, but then everything stops. This morning was significant. I woke up and played solitaire in bed, contemplating my plans for the day.

In the morning, I check my blood pressure and take my hormones. While doing that, I listen to the news on my Google bedside display. Then, I set up my pink exercise mat and used my Samsung Galaxy tab to do my exercises.

I follow a precise order of actions: brushing teeth, washing face, combing hair, and going to the kitchen for breakfast. Today, I deviated from my usual routine and skipped my morning exercise for no apparent reason. I pondered why, but sometimes a break in routine is necessary to reset.

2021/08/17 A Silent Cry

I took half a day off for a doctor's appointment today. After returning home, I watched stories of transgender people like me. Some made me laugh, others made me cry, seeing their struggles mirror mine.

Coming out early in life can result in acceptance or rejection from peers, family, or society, which can be challenging because of a lack of openness or understanding.

Today, while eating fish at my kitchen table, I watched one of my subscribed YouTube channels, Nikki Tutorials: Layers of Me. A heartwarming tale of a trans woman, who began early in life, recounting her path to where she is now. Embraced and accepted by her mother, I wish my situation mirrored this, but like most people in my situation, wander through life, making sense and longing for freedom.

I'm at a breaking point, questioning my gender. Why am I male instead of female? Hoping to transform into a beautiful woman overnight, like a dream. Like a bird trapped, yearning to soar, yet that day seems distant.

Writing with tears streaming down my face, breaking free from gender dysphoria's grip. I am free to soar like a bird leaving the nest. I dream of the day I cry tears of joy, finally free to be me.

2021/08/18 Why So Early?

Getting enough sleep can be challenging. You go to bed at your usual time but end up waking up much earlier than expected. I need to complete my nightly routine by 11:00 p.m. Tonight differs from my usual sleep schedule.

I slept and woke up feeling like it was morning. I lay in bed, anticipating my 5:30 a.m. alarm. I checked the time on my Fitbit and realized it was 3:30 a.m. Despite my attempts, I couldn't sleep and restlessly waited until 4:48 a.m. I wondered why I was up so early as I wrote in my diary while I sat in bed.

2021/08/19 The Results are In

The test results from my last blood test were promising, but then I noticed something. Normal kidney function, liver enzymes, and electrolytes. The current state of estradiol levels shows they are still low.

My doctor suggested that I lower my cholesterol levels and prescribed a higher dose of Estradiol to increase my estrogen levels, which made me happy. Additionally, my doctor confirmed that all other results were good and did not provide any other suggestions.

2021/08/20 Why Did I Wait So Long?

This question often crosses my mind. Why did I hesitate before making this decision that would change my life? For nearly sixty years, I struggled with my identity, yearning to be a woman.

I've always had more female friends and loved being around women for their similarities to me, not physical attraction. I'm constantly surrounded by women in malls and markets, making me envision myself in their shoes.

Why did I wait so long to feel real? At 59, I contemplate my journey towards self-fulfillment as a woman.

The hormones are rearranging my brain and my body, and thinking again, why did I wait so long?

Many memories built over nearly six decades, the beginning for me. As most await life's end, I venture forth, leaving behind memories of loved ones. They've been to places, seen and done things while I wonder, why did I wait so long?

It's a tough question, but I'm sure the long wait had a reason. You know, waiting for the right time was worth it to make my dreams a reality.

Today, I began taking an additional dose of Estradiol, at 2mg, one dosage higher than before, in hopes that it will elevate my estrogen levels and help me embody the woman I aspire to be.

2021/08/21 F&D Day *(Father and Daughter Day)*

Today I decided to step out of the house on what would have been a planned day to go check out a mobile home I'm thinking of buying and living my new life as a woman, but plans don't always work out the way you want.

I called my daughter to tell her I'll drop off a package she ordered and then head to a mobile home lot in Kennesaw.

Instead, it turned into what I call an F&D Day. I delivered the package to my daughter and then decided to take her to Sandy Springs to show her a shortcut back home.

In Sandy Springs, we visited her workplace, which is across from my office. Then, we went to Einstein Beagles for hot chocolate and beagles.

After that, we headed back to Marietta where she lives in a three-bedroom apartment shared with a friend but before that, we stopped by Hobby Lobby' at the empty parking lot and spent the next hour teaching her how to drive a car with a manual transmission.

When she was 17, I taught her how to drive an automatic car, a 2016 Chevrolet HHR. I had no other vehicle at that time. Later, when her brother learned to drive, I had a car with a manual transmission.

I had wanted to teach her, but she wasn't interested. Now that she is, I really enjoyed our time together. Then, I dropped her off at her apartment and went to see the mobile home in Kennesaw. The entrance is impressive, with a large wooden sign that said "Woodlands at Kennesaw" in big letters.

As I drove through the place, I noticed it appeared to be a mixed community with many single and double-wide mobile homes, both old and new. However, the one I'm looking for is not on the lot because it is still under construction. I'm looking forward to seeing it on September 9th at 10:00 a.m.

2021/08/23 Why am I So Sleepy?

Each day is almost identical to the one before. As I progress with my transition, I get out of bed, monitor my blood pressure, take my hormones, and exercise for thirty minutes. I feel great and everything seems to fall into place. I have been feeling tired and sleepy lately. Why do I feel tired all day despite feeling rested and energized in the morning?

2021/08/25 Terrible Timing

In a time of this horrible pandemic that just keeps developing COVID-19 and COVID-19 DELTAV, what's its next evolution? You can't help to think of it whenever you get sick, you take every precaution to protect yourself such as wearing a mask wherever you go which it's often easy to forget.

Upon arriving at your destination, you notice masked faces as you approach the door. People of all ages, genders, and the occasional mask refusers complicate matters for others.

Mask-wearing faces prompt a U-turn to put on your mask. I've gotten compliments for my mask, a colorful one kind of like the PRIDE flag. I never imagined seeing this on a global level.

When you catch a mild cold, COVID is always on your mind. Last night, I got a slight cold. I wore a sleeveless one-piece outfit with spaghetti straps and felt cold from the air conditioner. I ignored it, but now I have a sore throat and runny nose in the morning. Don't worry though!

I got vaccinated months ago, so I'm sure it's not COVID. The refusal to wear masks by ignorant individuals prolongs the pandemic and increases the death toll.

2021/08/26 A Good Night's Sleep

A good night's sleep made a difference. I felt a touch of the flu for two days, but today I woke up feeling a little better. Being sick doesn't immediately compel me to take medicine or anything else. Sure, it may feel refreshing and soothing, but nothing compares to the pure, crystal-clear sensation of a cool, quenching cup of water.

Drinking more water when sick improves health and enhances end-of-day well-being. It causes frequent urination, but sweating helps fight the cold and you'll feel better in the morning. Let's see how the day unfolds.

As the day went on, I grew sleepy and took a half day off work. After a quick nap, I spent the rest of the day relaxing. In the evening, I cooked a delicious Japanese curry, which I haven't made in a while.

2021/08/2 HRT Update

After four months on HRT, my breasts feel full but there's no noticeable tissue development, only increased volume. It's been a month since I last measured. The measurement reduced from 45" to 44 1/2". It is completely normal for women to experience monthly fluctuations in their breasts.

I polish my fingernails in a soft clear pink color, a shade darker than my natural nails, and aim for a feminine appearance when going to the doctor's office. It is enjoyable for me to engage in the coordination of colors. Last time I went to my doctor's office for my appointment, I wore green fleece pants and green tunic with my toes and fingernails in a hunter green and brown three-inch heel and I got compliments. While working from home today, I wore blue and white striped pants, a tunic, and blue polished nails.

2021/08/28 An Exciting Day

My first evening Zoom meeting with a transgender group was overwhelming and emotional, but it made me realize I'm not alone.

At the Podiatrist

Last week, I saw my podiatrist for issues with my right foot. Based on my x-ray analysis, the podiatrist advised me to get supportive shoes from a footwear company.

Two weeks ago, I went to Georgia Peach Running Company in Kennesaw. I wore a light green t-shirt, gray pants, black slip-on shoes, and had a women's wallet and sunglasses with rhinestones.

I walked into the store and two young women asked if I needed help. One named Tammy and the other Amy. My shirt read a funny message that said. Don't worry, I've already had my two shots.

The shirt had shot glasses and a lemon slice at the bottom, which started a conversation. I showed them a note from my podiatrist and told Amy I needed specific footwear. Their willingness to assist us was greatly appreciated.

Both women brought out shoe boxes with men's and women's shoes in neutral colors. I tried on several pairs and settled on black New Balance shoes in size 11 wide.

While talking to them, I confidently introduced myself as Tamara. They treated me well, calling me by my name. I left feeling satisfied, wearing new women's walking shoes and a big smile.

2021/08/29 The Last Three Days

Last Thursday I woke up with a sore throat but I thought nothing about it till noon that day. Feeling sleepy and tired, I took a half-day off from work. The day flowed on Friday, but I started feeling sick again at night.

I went to bed early and thought I had COVID on Saturday morning, but I don't have a fever or typical symptoms of the virus that has caused widespread devastation.

Despite being fully vaccinated with Pfizer months ago, I couldn't get tested because of all appointments being taken. Having only a slight cough and headache, I knew it wasn't the virus, so I waited. Surprisingly, the flu caught me off guard after years of wellness, but thankfully I recovered on day three.

2021/08/30 Take a Deep Breath

Today, I woke up without coughing or sniffing for the first time in days. I beat the cold and I'm feeling better and ready for the day. No flu symptoms will interrupt my exercise routine. I'm feeling energized, and my breast plumped and jumping off my chest, something I had not felt in the past few days. It's amazing how your body reacts to minor changes based on your health and state of mind.

2021/08/31 Well Rested

Finally, I woke up feeling refreshed after being sick for a few days. As the morning dawned, I opened my eyes at 5:00 a.m. Just fifteen minutes later, I eagerly got out of bed to start my day.

2021/09/01 4th Quarter

As the calendar turns to the fourth quarter of the year, anticipation fills the air, tinged with a hint of excitement and hope. I eagerly await the next four months, envisioning a brighter 2022 where I will emerge like a butterfly from its cocoon, ready to unveil my authentic self to the world.

2021/09/03 Busy Weekend

Today will be my usual morning routine, but the weekend will be busy. My start time is 10:00 a.m. on Saturday. Appointment at 1:00 p.m. in Kennesaw to see a new mobile home. I have plans to see a car with my daughter and then go for a walk with an LGBT group at the park on Sunday, which will be my first outdoor event since COVID.

2021/09/04 Busy Day

I have two events on my calendar today. The first one is finally seeing the mobile home I have been hoping to buy, and I hope the payments are not high.

At 1:00 p.m., I have an appointment with my daughter to check out the car she plans to buy. I hope her approval goes through. Lunch will be somewhere in between.

2021/09/05 Another Busy Day

Yesterday was busy, I missed a virtual meeting with an LGBT support group because I was visiting dealerships with my daughter in Smyrna. She had a 1 p.m. appointment with a sales associate.

He was a nice and honest person from Mexico, but the 2016 Chevrolet Malibu she wanted had cosmetic issues. She considered a 2016 Ford Fusion hybrid on the same lot, but we decided to go to another dealer.

When we arrived at the second Chevrolet dealer lot in Marietta, just 10 minutes north of Smyrna, an accident occurred on the highway in front of the dealer. A tire had fallen off the back of a pickup truck that was loaded with tires and traveling north on Highway 41.

The police car blocked the area to prevent an accident while a man retrieved the tire.

As we pulled into the dealer's lot, salesmen gathered outside. A handsome gentleman approached us, and my daughter discussed her specifications with him.

He showed her a 2018 Chevrolet Sonic at a good price, but she disliked its performance and found it too small.

Then we visited our final dealer, a CarMax about 25 minutes north. However, they had nothing of interest for her, so we went home and that was our day.

2021/09/06 Another Day Another Test Drive

My daughter came early from Marietta, Georgia for our car test drive appointment at 9:00 a.m. We left the house at 10:15 a.m. for our first test drive in Chamblee, after having breakfast and coffee.

We arrived early, but the car dealer was unprepared. While he was with another customer, my daughter and I went to an oriental-themed shopping center with various businesses and restaurants.

We ate at an expensive Korean restaurant, but the food was worth it. After finishing our meal, we went to the sales lot.

The 2016 Hyundai Sonata had cosmetic issues with its metallic blue paint and peeling clear coat. The seats inside were dirty, but I reassured my daughter it wasn't a big deal. The center compartment between the front seats had broken, and the driver's seat was misaligned and non-adjustable, which made it impossible for my daughter to reach the pedals. It was a big disappointment.

We went back to Smyrna and found a small dealership with newer, well-maintained models. She test drove a 2018 silver Chevrolet Malibu, which drove like a charm.

After returning, she viewed another black Malibu hybrid. Since the brakes were too sensitive for her, she asked me to drive it. I fell in love with the hybrid Malibu, but she wanted to test another car before making a final choice.

2021/09/08 Last Shopping Day

My daughter and I have been driving around town for days looking for the right car, and she believes she has found it. She has been working hard researching cars and dealer ratings and has done all the work to find the perfect car at the right price.

Today is the last shopping day. She has an appointment to see a 2013 Hyundai Sonata GLS in Carlton, Georgia. I hope the car is worth the drive, otherwise, we'll go back to Smyrna for the Malibu we tested.

We drove into the dealer's lot and got the keys for the dark blue Hyundai Sonata.

The car was appealing both from a distance and up close, despite minor nicks and scratches. It was clean, well-maintained, and the test drive sealed the deal.

2021/09/09 Get Rid of It

My transition has been going well, albeit slow. I've noticed mood changes, breast growth, slower body hair, and improved memory.

I've been hesitant to talk to my wife and kids about my transition due to the fear of the unknown. I exhibit feminine behavior such as caring for my appearance, including my hair and nails. I can no longer hide the growth of my breasts and need to start wearing a proper bra.

2021/09/10 A Quiet Time

Today was a quiet day at work. I worked on cases and had two internal support calls. I also had a lunch meeting with The Loft an LGBT support group on Zoom. The meeting was deeply impactful, especially when discussing 9/11/01.

Where was I on that day? I was driving 18-wheel rigs at the time transporting trailers of auto parts for a Nissan assembly plant in Merryville TN on that day I had just approached the TN state line driving north on I-75 from Atlanta to Nashville.

As I crossed the state line, I tuned into 92.9, a radio station from Chattanooga TN. The news anchor interrupted the music with a special bulletin, announcing the first airplane's collision with tower one.

No one suspected a terrorist attack on US soil. The news deteriorates quickly as the second tower was struck and suspicions of a terrorist attack arise.

The day felt like an eternity to reach home. The run from Nashville to Atlanta used to take me eight hours, but that day felt much longer. I came home to find my wife watching the news. Overwhelmed, I fell to my knees in tears as I witnessed the horror unfold before me. This was the longest day ever as I witnessed the horror unfolding.

2021/09/11 Why Am I Up This Early?

I woke up at 5:00 a.m. feeling rested and ready for the day. Today is 9/11 remembering that day of the terrorist attack in New York, Pennsylvania, and Washington, DC. I didn't lose any family or friends, but nonetheless, the lives lost are painful enough. Even after twenty years, it still feels like it happened today, and my heart goes out to everyone who lived through it or didn't make it.

2021/09/12 Rise'n Shine

Some days, you wake up thinking it's time to get out of bed, only to realize it's thirty minutes earlier. Upon waking up, you glance at the time and realize it's early and you fall back to sleep. It's ten minutes before your alarm goes off. I feel well despite my sleep being interrupted earlier than expected.

2021/09/13 Moving Forward

Two months until my next evaluation with my doctor for my transition from M2F. I'm acting more like a female in some ways and my voice is changing and skin is softer though I'm still growing facial hair but is slower than usual. My body is going through noticeable changes, with my breasts and hips growing bigger over time.

2021/09/14 Where Would I Be?

Where would I be if I transitioned earlier and didn't have my current responsibilities? I'm at a point in my life where transitioning from M2F is the next step. This is what kept me from transitioning earlier on.

When the children are grown and more capable of taking care of themselves, at which point do you decide to take that important step in your life to transition from the responsibilities of financial stability and family?

Today, I am finally here. This is the moment I've longed for. If not for this stage in life, I would have realized my true gender sooner.

Now is the time and I'm ready to move forward to be Tamara. The woman in the mirror is breaking through. My dedication to a cause has been unwavering, as time shapes one's perspective.

2021/09/15 Why Am I Sad?

Yesterday I was feeling good. The first thing after my morning routine, I prepared for an appointment with my podiatrist for problems with my right foot because of tendinitis.

So, I wore gray wide-leg pants and a light green top with a funny message that said, "Don't worry, I already had my two shots." I arrived at the appointment on time at 8:00 a.m. After a twenty-minute wait, I was next as the door to the patient's area opened.

Ellie, my podiatrist, smiled and complimented the humorous message on my shirt after examining my foot and we both had a laugh. That made me feel good.

Today was a completely different story, I woke up earlier at 5:00 a.m, and after playing my usual game of Microsoft Solitaire I sat in my bed thinking and suddenly I broke down in tears. I experienced a moment of overwhelming thoughts for about five minutes. I pondered the reason for my sudden sadness.

Despite believing it had ended, I cried twice before lunch. I broke down in tears once more, two days later. It had a meaningful purpose, even if it seemed stupid at the time.

I'm the only one in my household who works from home and spends the day alone. I have to plan a meal for my wife, son, and me. They arrive home at 7:00 p.m. By then dinner is done, but two hours before they come home, I rush to decide and cook the meal, leaving me more exhausted than an eight-hour workday.

On September 16, I cooked beef tips with vegetables and a spicy Caribbean Jerk sauce. I take pride in my cooking and hope my family enjoys the fresh hot meal.

My wife always complains and nothing positive ever comes out of her mouth, so it wasn't surprising that she ruined this day too.

She came home and walked into the kitchen and saw the pan sitting on top of the stove, her first reaction was to complain about the pot I used since it was bigger than the food it held, and that started a list of complaints from her when I expected a thank you.

I anticipated praise, but her complaints overwhelmed me emotionally. She knocked on my door, entered after I gave permission, but the damage was done. I cried intensely for ten minutes.

2021/09/16 I'm Feeling Poetic Today

Using all 5 senses to describe someone I love, I would say…

Humans have unique ways of expressing emotions through our five senses: touch, sight, smell, taste, and hearing.

1st is the sense of touch: Touching is one of the most beautiful of the human senses, this is how we communicate and engage in our world and our relationships if I had no other way to say I love you I would touch you every day with my hands to tell you how much I love you, how much I care and will do all that I can to be with you, my love.

2nd is the sense of sight: With my sight, I'm able to see a world full of colors as lovely as nature can express, with my sight I would tell you that my heart belongs only to you my love and there is nothing else in this world between you and I to keep us apart.

3rd is the sense of smell: I can smell the flower's scent and the morning wind and if this was the only sense I had to interact with the world, I would live using this gift to follow every step you take like a hummingbird seeking the most succulent flower to perch on and take in the sweet nectar of your essence and follow you till my heart no longer beats to your scent.

4th is the sense of taste: It's a wonderful human pleasure to be able to taste the sweet and bitter fruit and if this was the only way I could express my feelings for you my love I would live tasting your skin like a sweet tangerine citrus and savor the moment as long as you are by my side and would cherish every moment with you, my love.

5th is the sense of hearing: If I could only use my hearing I would use it like an eagle seeking his prey in the shadow of night to follow your path and keep close to you, if all I could do is hear you I wouldn't be too far from your heart and be close to you till my last breath and let you know that your heartbeat is all I live for.

If all our senses could speak it would be like an orchestra of expression creating a beautiful melody and we would not be the same without all our senses, such as an orchestra wouldn't be the same without a pianist.

2021/09/17 A Day at The Service Center

I had an appointment today at the Hyundai dealership for two recalls on my 2012 Hyundai Veloster. They needed to do a software upgrade and replace the air compressor in the tire inflation kit.

This morning, I coordinated my outfit with green nails, a green top, and a green Fitbit band. I also wore a necklace with a gold and black pendant before heading to the dealer.

I drove into the service bay after they checked my car in. I was told it would take about four hours, so today will be the longest time I spend in public dressed as a woman.

The dealer served me competently and respectfully, regardless of my gender, providing a satisfactory experience.

2021/09/19 So Much Rain

The skies have had a major overflow since early morning, with heavy rain expected throughout the day.

I'm just sitting and relaxing. I fixed my wife's computer, which had a hijacked browser displaying the language in Check. I changed the language to Japanese to work on restoring it to English.

I was able to change it back to English, but the tabs and page continues to display in Check. I attempted to restore the browser settings, but it remained unchanged. I decided it's time for drastic measurements to restore the computer to factory settings since it's running slow. It will keep me occupied for a while.

Restoring a computer to factory specifications is time-consuming but worth it for a computer running like new. Reinstalling software and downloading files takes time after formatting.

2021/09/20 Bold Step Forward

Life occasionally calls for a major jump. Crying is a release as I embrace the courage to make my voice heard and shed my burdens.

I wrote a letter to HR, requesting a name and gender identity change as a transgender woman. Tears flow, knowing that everything is falling into place.

2021/09/21 Up So Early?

When you sleep, you wish to either sleep till sunrise or wake up to your alarm. Last night this was me, I usually go to sleep at about 11:00 p.m. but last night I got in bed early, and after my night routine of a twenty-minute exercise, taking my hormones, checking my blood pressure, the usual self-care steps.

I went to bed at 10:30 p.m. Despite my efforts to create a conducive sleep environment, I couldn't sleep all night. I woke up at 3:30 a.m and couldn't fall back asleep, so I played Solitaire on my phone. I fell asleep and woke up at 5:30 a.m.

2021/09/22 Day of The Big Reveal Day 1

Today I'm waking up with a big step in my transition. Earlier this week I searched online for sample letters to announce my "coming out" to my employer.

I found plenty of letters and after reading a few samples I found the perfect letter. The letter came from a WordPress article from Lives in Transition, the letter title was obviously eye-catching Coming Out so it couldn't have been clearer, after reading the letter I downloaded it to Microsoft Word and began to edit it to suit my purpose.

It took about thirty minutes of my time and after proofreading my own words I took the next step, send to self. I sent the letter to my work email at Cox Automotive and from there it took me several minutes thinking about the click-to-send button to my Corp Sr. HR representative at 12:12 p.m. And then I clicked on send, there is no turning back from here.

I was nervous and worried for all the wrong reasons, it seemed like it took a long time for her to respond but nearly 3 hours later at 2:54 p.m. she responded and her response was positive and supportive and two days later she set up a meeting with me to talk and offered to help me with resources and anything that she can do as I transition.

I could not have been much happier knowing that my employer is very supportive, and I can feel free to talk.

Meeting with HR

I just had a meeting with the HR for Cox and I felt so welcomed and it was a great experience. The next step is to change my email address to Tamara and change my gender pronouns to she, her & here's. One step at a time coming together.

2021/09/23 Day of The Big Reveal Day 2

Today I received an email from a case sent to the support team that changed my first name from Tomas to Tamara, this was faster than I expected and the first clue that it was completed was when I refreshed the page I was working on and I noticed that my name now reads Tamara Rivera.

Many programs on the header received the updates, but bumps are often experienced. My team members noticed the updates on the systems that were updated right away, and at least one team member asked if I had changed my name.

It happened quickly, leaving me unprepared to answer questions. All I managed to say was there will be a team meeting later.

2021/09/24 What a Day!

Today I logged in to work as usual by five minutes to 8:00 a.m. and with much anticipation for good news to see my name Tamara to be finally registered across all systems but that was not the case.

One of the key systems that I need was still unavailable, and I began looking for emails and messaging for responses from cases to see what was going on.

To my disappointment, the first message I read was not positive. To my disappointment, I read the first message, which stated an unwanted submission error had occurred in changing my name from Tomas to Tamara.

I experienced a break in all systems because I didn't have the provision for the name change, and the message instructed me to continue using my formal name.

It made me deeply sad and angry. I couldn't resist sobbing, overwhelmed with a sense of defeat as if it signaled the end.

I messaged my manager to inquire about the reason. Would they still require my formal name if I legally changed it?

I also shared with her the response and kickback received, and she said that she was going to talk to Carl, the support technician that sent me the message.

My manager has been supportive since I shared with her I'm coming out as a transgender woman, and I would not have such a supportive manager had it been anyone else.

Thirty minutes later, I received an email informing me that my name had been updated in the key systems I needed. After restarting my computer, I experienced a sense of relief as I saw my name, Tamara, updated in all systems. I finally felt a sense of accomplishment and satisfaction.

I am grateful for the support and acceptance of my longtime friends from COX Automotive.

2021/09/25 Day of The Big Reveal Day 3

My life has been changing rapidly, and I've discussed my transition with my manager twice in the past three weeks. I spoke to another friend who advised me to talk to the HR manager. It was encouraging to see that the response I received was positive.

My next step is my family and I find it difficult to talk to my wife, I have tried and had been thinking in my mind for weeks that today is the day. I have been holding back my voice and this morning I woke up at 3:30 a.m. and wrote an email to her, with tears in my eyes.

Here is what I wrote to her.

> From: Tomas Rivera
> To: Yasuko Rivera
> Subject: Let's talk
>
> Yasuko, I've been wanting to talk to you for a while, but fear holds me back. I respect you and really appreciate you and I really care but I find it difficult to approach you I have to tell you what's in my heart.
>
> I'm tired of living behind the walls and my life is going through a lot of changes, and I can't continue hiding from you and the world.
>
> I love my kids with all my heart, and they also deserve to know the truth. This is hurting a lot, but we have to talk and I just don't even know how to start.
>
> Sent via the Samsung Galaxy A71 5G, an AT&T 5G smartphone

2021/09/25 I got up early as usual and was tired since I had not slept well last night, after taking my blood pressure and the hormones I sent a text to my wife alerting her to read the email I sent to her earlier in the morning.

She was still sleeping when I got up and I headed to the kitchen and as I sat there drinking a cup of coffee she walked into the kitchen and I asked her if she had read the email I sent to her.

She looked at her phone and read the text I sent her, and she opened Microsoft Outlook to read the email and her reaction was cold, but why would I expect anything else?

She is not soft-hearted as I am and is cold and her comments are like a rock hitting you in the face. She's a nice person but her character is typical of a Japanese cold and expressionless. I sat, coffee in hand, seeking compassion but tasted bitterness instead.

Later today my son was sitting in the living room filling out a student loan application to refinance his current loan and there he was hoping to hear words coming out of my son's mouth be hard and bitter but all I heard was that it does not matter. I am transgender he replied that he already knew that and that he did not have a problem with it.

Later that day, I was outside using an air blower to clean the grass clippings off the driveway while my daughter drove in. I greeted her and then finished cleaning.

I sat at the porch table with my daughter, took a sip of water, and told her I am a transgender woman. She assured me she already knew and was okay with it, putting my fears to rest. My wife remained calm when she saw our children's calm response, which made me feel good about their acceptance.

2021/09/26 What's My Next Step?

This morning, I woke up refreshed and started my day with a game of solitaire on my phone while listening to Google News. I'm overwhelmed by the speed of my transition.

Within a week, I came out to my manager, the HR team at Cox Automotive, and my family.

What's my next step? What is the time and cost involved in legally changing my name? How can I update it in all my legal paperwork?

2021/09/27 Tamara's first Day

Finally, I embrace the first full day of being recognized as Tamara Rivera, a name that represents my true self and brings me immense happiness.

My birth name is now sitting on the sidelines for a moment, my next step is to change it legally. It may not be easy due to document changes, but I'm happy that Tamara is now a real person, not an image in my mind.

Today I'm having a company meeting to reveal my gender identity and new name. I'm excited, like a dragonfly emerging from its larvae state for the first time, with vibrant colors and energy.

2021/09/29 A New Day for Tamara

Today I woke up to a renewed sense of being me. I've been wanting to dye my hair for a while now. I've thought about different colors, but I want to avoid blonde and other light shades. I prefer dark tones that match my style, but I'm not sure which color specifically.

I spent a long-time window shopping, making it difficult to choose the right color. At Walmart, I debated between L'Oreal's deep red and Splat Rebellious Colors. I purchased Crimson Obsession and waited two months before dyeing hair.

Bleaching was necessary for my natural dark brown hair to follow the instructions. The bleach turned my hair blond, but it looked weird. I washed it off after thirty minutes to eliminate residue.

Applying the color was easy, but I noticed light and dark tones after washing my hair. My hair got damaged by the bleach when I missed some areas while doing it for the first time.

Today, virtually at work, there were four consecutive meetings with phone coordinators I've known since 2008. The meeting included the newest members for a minimum of five years.

There were 6 to 10 people per meeting, and I introduced myself as Tamara. They were supportive and happy. During the final meeting, I was flooded with emotions and teared up. It was incredible to see my true friends so happy for me. This is just the beginning of my new life as Tamara.

2021/10/01 What is the meaning of a friend?

I had to search for the meaning of friendship to define it. Friends can be unpredictable, alternating between love and disappointment.

It was not till after I woke up and took the courage to reveal my transition as a transgender that I realized how many loving friends I had. Unexpectedly, I received congratulatory calls for coming out.

I had to ask Google what a friend is, and here's its response.

A True Friend Has Your Back When others try to hurt you emotionally or physically, they do everything they can to make sure you stay safe. They don't care who is trying to harm you; they will defend you anytime, anywhere. If they can help you, they'll do it without reservation or reward.

I received a surprising call last night from someone who used to work at Cox years ago. Just when you think someone is no longer your friend, it turns out that you are mistaken. A real friend remains loyal through time and life's changes.

He left the company years ago; we worked alongside each other in a support group of four as online coordinators for Cox Automotive for at least three years. We built memories throughout that time; he has many talents such as I, and he is also a photographer.

I started my acting career as an extra in a few movies and he helped me build a profile. Since he left the company, I hadn't talked to him. Yesterday, I realized he's a genuine friend who has my back.

2021/10/02 Obstacles to Overcome

I'm thrilled to have more friends and accomplishments in a short time, despite the obstacles. The most important thing is financial stability, but I haven't reached that point yet.

As I sit here at my kitchen table having breakfast. How to raise the funds I need to take control of my finances and see my dreams come true? Is it too late for my transition at nearly sixty years of age?

They say you are never too old to take that step but then as I sit here, I'm also thinking of establishing a foundation for transgender people which may help me and countless others who suffer and endure so much pain and humiliation to the point of breaking down and doing the unthinkable.

I believe I'm strong and have plenty of courage, confidence, and determination to see my dreams come true as I stand for what I so strongly believe in but I know that is not the case for many other transgenders out there from murder-suicide and drug overdose is only a handful of issues affecting a community of millions.

Many struggle to fit in a society that does not accept their chosen gender. Raising a foundation of awareness to help others from the young and old male or female or whatever the choice may be in the LGBTQIA+ community, I aspire to be an ally to those in need of help and support.

So what's next? Where do I go from here?

2021/10/02 At the Hair Salon

Today is my first visit to a hair salon. A few days ago, I attempted to dye my hair crimson red as a DIY project, but the results were not good. I ended up with a patchwork of red, pink, and black. It looked weird, and I was not satisfied with the results.

At 1:45 p.m., the pizza and hot wings arrived. I had two slices and two wings in the living room with my kids. I departed from my house at approximately 2:15 in the afternoon.

I drove over to Canton, Georgia to a Dominican hair salon, I arrived 10 minutes to 3:00 p.m. and there were three women getting their hair done and I was next in line. While I waited I was browsing women's articles on my Google phone, one of the three women working there called me to have me sign in and fifteen minutes later they called out Tamara.

I took my turn on the black chair, one of three in the salon. The salon has a front waiting area, a registration station with an iPad and three chairs for clients. On the right side, there are hair dryers, and beyond that, there are hair washing stations. The small salon had women working there, all of whom were Spanish and from the Dominican Republic. The ambient energized me with the typical salsa music of the three sister islands of Cuba, Dominican Republic, and Puerto Rico, and I was enjoying it.

I didn't get the name of anyone there so I'm going to name the woman that worked on my hair Mercedes since the name of the salon was Mercedes Dominican Hair Salon. After she asked me what I wanted done to my hair she placed a black vinyl drape over my shoulders and a few minutes later she came back with a handmade mix of creams.

I saw her mix on a table in the back room and she came back to apply it on my hair, that was the color remover to clean out the crimson red off my hair and I sat there for about 20 minutes and she checked twice prior to leading me to the back to the hair washing station.

She took me to the chair and applied the color. Since it was my first time in a salon, I didn't understand the process and she didn't say much, so I just followed her instructions. Moments later, I went back to the hair washing station and sat in a different black chair on the left side of the room.

The time came for the last step: blow-drying my hair, applying a treatment, trimming the ends, and combing my hair. Once she finished, it was time for the mirror. I sat there, facing the mirror, and didn't recognize myself with red hair.

2021/10/06 Where Do I Go Next?

The answer usually comes to me as I walk along on my journey as a transgender woman. Two weeks since coming out, everyone has applauded my courage. I'm constantly wondering what my next move is.

2021/10/07 A Quiet Day

Today I had a busy day at work. Morning support calls flowed smoothly but significantly slowed by noon, enabling uninterrupted work in the quiet afternoon.

After work while I was cooking, I was on a Zoom meeting with one of the LGBTQIA+ support groups that I subscribe to. This group was new to me, and it was two hours long but I met more people that are in the same or similar situation as I.

A bearded man, like other transgender individuals, felt trapped by life's obstacles. I sympathized with them, as this is a common experience for most transgender people.

2021/10/08 On the Wrong Side of the Bed

This morning, I woke up to what seemed like a typical day. I got up and did my morning routine and about an hour later I started to get a runny nose, watery eyes, sneezing, and a slight fever, while I was working. During this ongoing pandemic, even the slightest flu symptoms make you consider COVID.

I worked until lunch and took a quick nap, feeling better afterwards. A difficult client, who was verbally abusive and constantly complaining, tested my patience later in the day.

I help my company clients, but this guy was abusive, so I shut him out by taking off my headset. I allowed him to hang up after refusing to listen to his abuse.

This put me to the brink of a nervous wreck and I for one had it and all I could do was cry after he hung up. I wanted to give him a piece of mind, but I was not going to let him get the worst out of me.

I'm better than that and my job means a lot to me. I called one of my friends and shared the experience with him but I was in tears and had trouble talking, he's a bug guy with a gentle heart and he calmed me down and made me feel better. I called my manager, in tears and feeling hurt. But our conversation made me feel better. By the end of the day, I felt better than in the morning.

2021/10/10 Clothing Dilemma

I've been wearing black women's bottoms and men's tops for six months to avoid upsetting my partner.

Since I came out as transgender three weeks ago, my kids have become more accepting, but she still holds traditional beliefs and can't accept it. She took a week off in September; but I stuck to my routine.

I start my day with exercise, hormones, breakfast, and coffee. I change into my chosen outfit for work each day, alternating between a colorful flowery top and a solid bottom. I wanted her to know that since my coming out, I'm no longer going to hide behind closed doors.

While walking down the main hall, she conveyed her disapproval of my fashion choices through her facial expressions. I changed my daily fashion during the week and felt everything was going well, but by Wednesday she claimed I looked like I'm putting on a fashion show every day.

I entered my office, which was once my daughter's room, and closed the door. I don't know if her comment was a criticism or a compliment.

Today after I woke up, I was looking at my dresser through the top three drawers where I have tops, pants, and other outerwear items deciding what to wear, by now I'm tired of the old black-on-black or solid-color men's T-shirts I've been wearing.

Women's fashion celebrates our natural beauty with colorful designs and intricate lace details, giving us many options to choose from. Women have a wide range of options to express their style, from tops with different sleeve lengths to pants, skirts, and dresses of various lengths. In contrast, men's fashion sticks to more subdued tones, offering less variety for personal expression.

2021/10/10 Another First

Today, I spent most of the day dressed as a woman, which was an exciting experience. In the morning, I started searching for a hair salon but unexpectedly found myself at a Sally Beauty store, where the wide variety of beauty supplies impressed me.

Though I didn't spend much time browsing, I did have a brief, pleasant conversation with a young woman at the counter. Since I was short on time, I left the store and headed to an Ulta Cosmetics just a few doors down.

I didn't intend to buy anything, but I wanted to find a nail polish to match a pink color I liked. While washing my hair, the red dye bled onto my nails, and that's when I met Stacy, a store consultant.

She was full body wearing jeans and a white blouse opened over her breasts, showing a tattoo spanning across her chest and a colorful tattoo on her left arm. She was a lovely young woman and had a friendly smile.

She helped me select a matching nail color by Opi in a delicate pink with a funny Spanish name called "Telenovela Me About It."

I also chose a clear enamel from Sally Hansen. I like this product since it has a soft wide brush that's easy to use and covers more of my nail with one stroke. She also answered all my questions on hair color and maintenance and suggested products to help keep my color longer and advised I set up an appointment to talk to their hair consultant and gave me a brochure with their services and pricing.

From there I walked up to the front counter where there was a beautiful dark-skinned woman to check out the nail enamel I chose and also signed me up for the free Ulta Beauty rewards card and told me the benefits of the card. I felt treated well by the staff at Ulta Beauty and left the store with a smile.

I left the shopping center and headed back home. I walked in and put my purchased items away, and sat in the living room, but I felt bored. Desiring more exposure as Tamara, I donned chic attire and set off. I visited a mobile home park and made a quick stop at Walmart on my way home.

I walked through the grocery aisles wearing women's clothing that hugged my body, making my breasts more noticeable. While shopping, I had to use the restroom. They had separate rooms for men, women, and families. I walked past the women's shoes and entered a room with restrooms and a layaway counter.

As I walked in, restrooms for men and women were on the left, and a mothers' room was on the right. I mistakenly assumed it was accessible to everyone, but a young woman clarified there was no bathroom there.

She knew I was not looking for a men's restroom based on my dress wear but she must have known that I was also not ready to walk into the women's bathroom and she said that I can use the one in front of me, which was for family. A feeling of relief washed over me. I finished my shopping and walked out with my head up high, feeling confident.

2021/10/14 What has changed?

I have been consistent in journaling for the past six months, but recently lost inspiration and skipped a few days, including the 11th and 13th of this month. I'm self-reflecting on what has changed.

What if I had fallen in love with my male therapist, my daily inspiration? Though the most significant change in my life has been having lost my free sessions with him. He being gay made our relationship difficult, but he inspired me to write daily in my diary. Now, where do I find inspiration?

I have new friends now and the newest one is a twenty-nine-year-old transgender woman from Texas whom I met from her reaching out to me privately through Slack, a technical support chat room used by all the technical teams in Cox Automotive, she was in the last LGBTQIA+ team meeting the company hosted and she offered to help me in any way she can since she has been also working on her transition.

I connected well with her and I can meet her if I can just make a trip to Texas. Could she be my new inspiration? We share similar interests and can support each other morally.

2021/10/15 Magdalena

Yesterday, my day began normally after my morning routine. I was ready to go to my office room across the hall from the main bedroom. After logging into my work computer, I started working on my cases but encountered an issue that shouldn't have been assigned to my team.

Since my team doesn't handle this issue, I reached out to the Manheim Credit and Collections HUB, who deal with financial matters. When I called, a powerful male voice answered. He was polite, but he assumed that the voice determines the gender.

Assumptions based on perception are terrible, but they shape our identity, which is mostly fine, but not today. I'm openly transgender and won't let anyone assume things about me in person or on the phone.

When I called, the receiver promptly addressed me as "sir" based on my perceived gender, which no longer applies. I let him continue and as the call came to his assurance that he was going to take care of it he again called me the dreaded word sir. The breaking point was when he did it twice, so I had to stop him and assert my pronouns as she/her. I suppressed my tears and ended the call on a sour note.

This was the beginning of a difficult day for me. It felt like a match had been struck, igniting a whirlwind of emotions in my mind. I found myself crying and sobbing at the slightest thing, with multiple moments throughout the day where I just couldn't hold back the tears.

All I wanted was to drop everything and log off work. I cried easily due to heightened estrogen levels, feeling akin to the weeping Magdalena from the Bible, which was an unpleasant experience.

2021/10/16 Unbelievable Support

I've been waiting for this moment for a long time. It feels like I've been trapped and unable to express myself, but now I'm finally free to explore new possibilities.

I took small steps like a mountain climber, step by step to the top, through the rocks that cut my flesh like a sharp blade. I made it unscathed but wounded by the past.

I spent much of my life hiding and denying my true self to those around me, constantly taking risks that someone might discover my love for wearing women's clothing. I couldn't comprehend my own mind at the time, but I often pondered my true identity.

I wanted to resemble the beautiful women in magazines. I envisioned myself wearing the beautiful clothes in the women's section of the department store, but I couldn't because of my fear of being discovered.

Breaking free from confinement, I was met with overwhelming support for my courage. Messages of love, acceptance, and encouragement were received from all over the US. Without breaching those four walls, I wouldn't have discovered new friends or my freedom.

2021/10/16 The positives and negatives of HRT

I've experienced physical and mental changes in hormone therapy for transitioning. I have observed both positive and negative outcomes, but mostly positive.

The positive impact can be summarized as follows:

1. Mood changes are more heightened; I'm more aware of things that before I would have ignored.
2. My libido has decreased significantly, which is important for my transition. Before HRT, I had a high sex drive and masturbated frequently. Despite being in my late fifties, I now have better control over my sex drive.
3. I am calmer and more in control. I am more talkative and sensitive towards others' feelings.
4. My skin has become more sensitive, so I shave gently with a woman's razor.
5. I prioritize myself and how I appear. I pay extra attention to my appearance before leaving my house.
6. I express my love for color through women's clothing. I love red and all shades of pink. I paint my nails pink and often decorate them with red roses.

HRT has blessed me with many positives, but there is only one thing I would consider a slight negative, if anything.

My emotional state is more on high alert, the slightest thing makes me cry and sometimes I don't even know why I'm crying while at other times it's for a reason, but I'm more sensitive to situations and people.

Tears filled my day on Wednesday this week. Everything was going flawlessly until a Google Photos memory of my kids from four years ago appeared on my phone as I was getting ready for my morning exercise routine.

There is an obvious difference between my kids' images from four years ago and today. My children's appearances have changed significantly. I cried while on my exercise mat but had to push through to workout.

Later, I sat at my desk in the room across the hall, my makeshift office during COVID-19. Memories played in my mind like a movie while I worked, causing me to cry multiple times. Despite the urge to quit, I stayed until the day ended.

2021/10/16 I Feel Validated

I felt validated wherever I went today. People were referring to me as ma'am and that alone made me feel happy. I demanded respect with my confident demeanor, makeup or not.

I wore a pink T-shirt with a V-neck, a gray sweater with wide cuffs, light gray pants with black stripes, and black slip-on shoes. I attempted to walk gracefully, with hip and hand coordination.

Popeye's Chicken was my first stop. I walked into the open dining room and the woman at the register asked, "What can I get you, ma'am?" In a kind tone, this acknowledged my gender for the first time.

I asked to speak with the manager about my complaint regarding a prior bad drive-through experience. She politely acknowledged and inquired about the details. She promised to handle the issue with her employees.

While I was at the soda fountain, a young woman delivered my order. They treated me with respect and acknowledged my gender.

Later, I visited Ulta Beauty, my go-to makeup store. I have been there three times, and the staff treated me well, acknowledging my gender. Validation of my gender through appearance and behavior is important to me.

2021/10/17 All Dressed up and No Where to Go

Things took a sudden turn for the worse after two weeks of preparation, leaving me feeling frustrated and without a purpose.

My friend canceled our plans last minute due to a family situation, and I reassured her that it was okay. It's now scheduled for next weekend.

I was looking forward to going to Chipotle for lunch this weekend as my first public outing as a woman with a close friend. I spent three hours preparing for the date, doing my makeup, finding the right outfit, and styling my hair.

Before leaving, I sent her another message requesting her address. I went to a Race Track gas station a few miles away. I wore multicolored wide-leg pants, a pink blouse, and a black rope necklace. My makeup took two hours and I thought it looked good. I refueled my car and went to Walmart on Thornton Rd for lip gloss.

I wore chunky-heel shoes, which I had not worn in two years since COVID-19, and this was my most embarrassing moment. I stumbled and struggled to maintain my balance as I approached the store entrance, drawing attention from onlookers. My friend canceled last minute again, leaving me feeling upset and foolish.

2021/10/18 The Worst Day Ever

Yesterday, my life's worst day. Got stood up, humiliated, looked horrible in high heels after two years. I underestimated the severity of the situation. My legs were sore as I walked around Walmart.

I held onto my remaining strength as I walked to my car. I hid by walking between parked cars, unable to take off my high heels since I didn't have spare shoes in my bag.

I keep flat shoes in my car for driving a manual transmission. My nice clothes were overshadowed by my humiliating stumbling in those shoes.

Does this mean no more high heels? Do I need to part away with my high-heel shoes? I love high heels, but I need to either retrain or give them up.

2021/10/19 Validated Full Circle

I have been on this journey to be recognized and respected by everyone including my brother and sisters as a transgender. I lived my whole life in hiding from the world, but today I wake up knowing that now my validation has come full circle.

The past month I have worked slowly to this moment and now it was time for either the love and support from my brother and sisters or their rejection.

Yesterday I cried so hard feeling lied to by a friend and my mind felt like a freight train of emotions I couldn't make sense of why I was let down by my best friend and my youngest sister Linda, I was ready for the worst and to my surprise I realized how wrong I was.

Many Christian people are quick to point fingers of judgment against you. If you feel differently, they are quick to cast you to the infernal hell. Instead of embracing Jesus' love, they opt for hate and inflict pain on others who don't fit their narrow perception of gender.

I called my sister Magali in Florida, knowing her love is unwavering. She's small in height but big-hearted with a gentle dose of love.

I was wrong to expect rejection. My sister's love touched me, regardless of what I expected. The Bible teaches in 2 Corinthians 13:13 that love is the greatest gift from God and is everlasting.

I didn't plan to call my siblings, expecting resistance and feeling emotionally shattered. As I called my third sister Madeline, not that she is the third since I didn't call them in order by age, but by which one I will feel the most rejection form. If any rejected me, it'd be my final call today.

I found it difficult to speak, causing me to hesitate before telling her. I felt empowered to come forward and reveal my authentic gender identity. I waited in silence for what felt like minutes. I got angry when she labeled it as a demon. I erupted like a volcano.

After those words hit me, I was determined not to let anyone, even my sister, speak to me that way. This was the response I expected of her and it should not have shocked me, but it did. and what came out of me were equally hurting words as if I was seeking revenge from her words. I hung up the phone after being told words of condemnation instead of love.

She texted me later with a more affectionate tone than anticipated. I'm so sorry my sincere apologies because I had no idea how to take this. I was speechless, but I have known about this our whole life. We never talked about it out of respect, but even Mom knew that does not make me love you any less. You are my big brother and will always be.

I was more shocked at your tone. We have never had such awful filth, and you address me disrespectfully. Please forgive me for what I caused you, I'm not used to that. I called her back and apologized. She responded with words of love and respect, even though she doesn't fully understand. She said she loves me and still considers me her brother.

I anticipated a similar response from Norma, who is the oldest of four sisters and five siblings. She has been through a lot and has been bruised and battered by life's cruel blows, but she still endures, and she respects me in her own way, she is a bit hard to talk to sometimes, but she is my sister and I love her.

Struggling to express myself, I quickly revealed, "I'm transgender. She responded quickly. She lovingly preached that she still loves me; love, not hate, is all I need.

My younger brother Tito, five years my junior, is as big as a gentle giant at six feet two inches tall, strong, and his reaction was unexpected.

As his older brother, I was unsure how he would react, but he still loved me just the same. I am open about my identity to friends and family and feel liberated.

2021/10/19 What is Happiness?

Happiness is a sought-after but seldom found treasure, concealed from many and discovered effortlessly by the fortunate few.

What is Happiness? Happiness is the context of a mental or emotional state, positive or pleasant emotions.

I searched high and low above the mountains and down in the valleys. No matter where I went, happiness remained out of reach.

Why is something, sought by everyone, so elusive? Am I using all the tools at my disposal to find happiness? Is it in the closet or garage? How about under the hood of the '55 Chevy? I never found it, by the big oak tree, as the old man said.

Neither a compass, nor Google maps, nor Siri could help me find happiness. If everything I tried failed, what is the solution?

I heard from an old lady aged in years withered and tattered by the passing time that I was looking in all the wrong places. What I'm looking for called happiness is a lot closer than I thought.

What is she talking about? I asked quietly to myself, if it's so close, why am I not finding happiness?

She observed my tired and confused glance, carrying a heavy burden. She read my thoughts with ease, leaving me speechless. With a confident gaze, she whispered secrets in a hushed manner. Her words resonated like a harp. What you seek is within you. Your heart is a sanctuary where happiness takes up residence.

021/10/20 Take A Step Back

I began my transition in May 2021 and have made progress since then. I must navigate obstacles and decide whether to go around or attempt to overcome them.

After sharing my transgender reveal with my sister Linda last night, her accepting response gave me the courage to inform the rest of my family. I felt completely validated.

I received rejection and disbelief from Linda when I opened up to her about my transition during our phone call the next morning. She thought it was a dream. I was Tomas my whole life, but now I am transgender and that is difficult for some to understand and accept. I am Tamara, a more secure and better version of myself who doesn't seek validation from others.

2021/10/21 Days of Wonder

On certain days, I wake up with a logical mind, while on others, I struggle with mental clutter and seek ways to regain focus.

It took me a month, but I've climbed up the chain to declare my identity as a transgender woman. Despite my strength and hope, I occasionally wake up feeling trapped, in need of an escape.

2021/10/21 My ideal bedroom

My dream bedroom is like a garden, with walls painted the color of the Blue Nile and a ceiling covered in shimmering star scenes, giving me a cosmic experience when I sleep.

The beautiful roses sitting on my dresser and makeup table fill my ideal bedroom with fragrances, so as I sit in front of the mirror, the aroma fills my senses and fills my heart with love.

My ideal bedroom feels like I'm outdoors in a garden amongst the birds, singing beautiful melodies as I smell the sweet fragrant flowers around me as I observe the wonders of nature that take me to worlds you can only dream of.

2021/10/22 Today I had an amazing time!

Once I finished my scheduled tasks, the hair salon provided the most satisfying experience. At Ulta Beauty, Sarah, the hairdresser, flawlessly achieved the desired color for my hair, despite the high cost of $130 plus an additional $30 for shampoo and hair gel. However, the outcome justified the expense, leaving me satisfied.

2021/10/23 Busy Schedule

I have a busy day ahead; I woke up at 5:00 a.m. today to plan my day out or rather to get ready for planned appointments.

I woke up, groomed myself, showered, and it was already 7:00 a.m. Shaving takes more time now because I use two razors - one for coarse hair and another for a smoother shave. Showering also takes longer, especially when I wash my hair.

8:00 a.m. Step outside and wash my car. I like to have a clean car and wash it once a week, but have not for two weeks and it's showing the dirt, so it's time for an overdue car wash.

10:00 a.m. My first appointment is with my therapist, Dr. Dorio, at 10:00 a.m., which usually takes about an hour, but not today. I will need to cut it short for my next event.

11:30 a.m. I have a scheduled lunch with my former manager at Cox back from 2008, when I first started working there. We developed a successful relationship with her, and to this day, we remain friends.

My third and last scheduled event is at 1:30 p.m. To a hair appointment with Ulta Beauty to recolor my hair to have the look I'm going for and complete my new personality.

2021/10/26 I Cried Myself to Sleep Last Night

Love from strangers has empowered me on this journey. I found some new friends at my local Ulta Beauty store from Miranda, the store manager. She's a successful, full-figured, beautiful young woman, tender and caring.

I talked to her a few times, she's a listener, and gave me successful hair care advice. Let's not forget about Sarah, who has gained a reputation for her exceptional skills as a hairdresser. She did an amazing job repairing and styling my hair, which I love and have received compliments on.

We had a great connection when she did my eyebrows. She shaped them perfectly and even recommended a product for my left brow.

The experience was great, receiving compliments from strangers made it worth it. But why did I cry last night despite all the positivity?

Breaking silence with my siblings has been an emotional roller coaster. Despite the hurtful expression, I won't seek revenge.

I visited my sister in Florida for a few days, but she struggles to accept and use my pronouns due to her religious beliefs.

Visiting my sister Magali in Florida, I found unconditional love and support from her and her daughters. I went out with her today, both of us dressed head to toe in women's clothing.

Happiness faded when bedtime arrived, and reality struck. She loved me like a sister, despite her difficulty using the correct pronouns and calling me Tamara.

I have no intention of pressuring or forcing her to call me Tamara. She delicately expressed her emotions, and as I laid down to sleep, I couldn't help but sob, reflecting on the painful rejection I experienced from my brother and younger sister.

2021/10/28 Amazing Day I'm Feeling So Loved

My nieces and nephews here call me Tia Tamara, which makes me happy to be their new aunt.

I changed my hair color and got my eyebrows done before coming from Georgia. Clairs in Florida. I got my ears pierced and wore small pink stud earrings. Getting my ears pierced on the way back to my sister's home filled me with happiness.

I enjoyed wearing high heels all day. I started the day with black and gray pumps, but while walking in them on my left foot, the shoes began rubbing on the side of my heel, rubbing into my skin and it hurt.

I walked barefoot on the asphalt parking lot, which was unusual for me since I never go without shoes.

I didn't want to stop, so I went back to my sister's home after making it to my car. I wore blue booties with rhinestones and a 3" heel. I had no issues walking around in them.

Then, I drove back to my sister's house where she was getting ready to go out. I planned to meet her ex-husband and introduce myself as Tamara.

We arrived at his home, and I met his new-wife from Mexico, a nice-looking elder woman with silver hair. We arrived in two cars to a restaurant and everyone had ice cream while I had a chicken salad and we had an exceptional time.

Two hours later, I was back at my sister's home where I sat in bed thinking of this day. Despite the discomfort in my feet at the end of the day, I persevered and wore heels and a nice outfit the entire day.

2021/10/29 A Day Dressed as Tamara

Since arriving at my sister's home in Florida, I have spent the entire day dressed elegantly as a woman, exploring various places. I shopped at Walmart with my sister, then ventured to Ulta Beauty and other places on my own, donning high heels and flawless makeup.

Each day, I learn more application techniques and add to my makeup collection, increasing the variety of products I have. I've gained more confidence and drastically changed as a woman.

2021/11/03 It's been a while since we last connected!

No entries in my journal since October 29th. This entry will be lengthy as a result of significant events.

My brother and other three sisters rejected me harshly, and it has been a while since my feelings were hurt.

Despite not receiving any replies, I'm certain they have reservations about my transition. This was expected, but why did they suddenly go from loving me one day to making me frown the next day?

I didn't expect this to affect my mind so deeply that I cried whenever I thought about it. I thought I was strong, but my emotions became a raging river of pain. I believe I'm stronger now and hope to better cope with this.

The last few days have been mixed with emotional and happy moments, so I elaborated on the latter and moved on.

It's been two weeks since I started dressing up as Tamara, with makeup, thanks to my sister Magali from Florida. As a result of recent experiences, I have noticed a significant increase in my self-assurance. Despite not using my preferred name or pronouns, she boosts my confidence and shows understanding and love.

2021/11/04 A Week Earlier

November 11 is my sixth anniversary since I started HRT M2F. However, I have asked my doctor for an earlier appointment so it was moved to one week earlier, which was today.

Two weeks ago, I was stressed. I'm more relaxed after a week off and looking forward to continuing my transition as a transgender woman. My blood pressure is good. I told the doctor how things were going after getting blood drawn and a flu vaccine.

I'm excited to increase my Estradiol prescription and possibly add progesterone for better breast development.

2021/11/06 What's in Store for Today?

Today was a dull day, sitting around in the chilly November weather. My niece Pricila called me through Zoom video this morning and I had a long chat with her for at least a couple of hours.

My daughter Katiya arrived quickly while I was talking to my niece and they also had a chat. After disconnecting from Pricila, I assisted my daughter in improving her resume for a job at COX Automotive, which I plan to share with Kim, the HR manager, with my team.

The rest of the day, we relaxed in the living room with my ex-wife, son, and daughter, watching a Teen Titans marathon. That's pretty much how our day went until 9:00 p.m.

2021/11/09 Discovering a New Passion

I've been exploring nail art for a couple of months, creating my own style and wearing a new design every week. Nail art fuels my passion for creativity and inspiration.

I logged into work at 8:00 a.m., but one of my applications would not allow me to login. Restoring my computer didn't solve the problem. I called the help desk and discovered that I couldn't log into my computer because I hadn't submitted a return-to-work note and was locked out.

Aetna told me to get a note from my doctor to unlock my access. I took care of personal affairs while waiting for reactivation.

2021/11/10 It's Official

Since I'm going to be off work due to a technical block, I have decided to take care of something I've been meaning to do. I looked online for legal advice to change my name and after consulting a lawyer and paying $60 for the consultation, they gave me a link to the application.

I completed the application online and later went to the Cobb County Superior Court in Marietta, Georgia to file a petition to legally change my name to Tamara. The court set a date for me to change my name to Tamara Rivera on December 30, 2021 at 9:30 a.m. So, starting January 1, 2022, I'll be celebrating the new year with my new name.

2021/11/11 Unwanted Time Off

Today is the second day since I got locked out of working by the FMLA group because of missing a return-to-work letter from my doctor's office. I'm new to this, I never had to do it before.

I have directed my attention elsewhere during this time. I found a post on Roomster.com to look for rooms for rent and I have found such a place; the rent is only $509 a month, and it's a pleasant house, so I'm looking forward to moving out and getting a room to myself to further explore my transition.

2021/11/13 Return to Work

I was absent from work for two days, but I made up for it by working overtime on Friday and two extra hours today. As a result, my team will start next week with no pending cases.

I had a meeting with my therapist, and I thanked Dr. Dorio for all that he has done for me these past few months. I appreciate his help and will rest until after the holidays. I wish to see him next year.

I asked my therapist to accompany me to court on December 30 for my name change hearing, but he can't make it due to work commitments.

I had a productive conversation with my wife today about our finances and we agreed on how to divide them after I move out.

2021/11/16 Who Can You Trust?

As a transgender woman, I've had many new experiences, both exciting and challenging. It's hard to trust people's words like I used to. I've spent a long time searching for rental rooms, but all I've encountered is discrimination, lies, deceit, and fraud.

A couple of months ago, I found a mobile home for rent in Kennesaw, Georgia. However, the manager didn't show up for a Sunday meeting and didn't respond to calls or texts. She responded after thirty minutes, lying about the place being unavailable during construction.

I wasted months using various rental apps without success. I used Roomster, a promising app with a good review on Google. I got a hit within 24 hours.

The location was near, and she appeared sincere. I felt something was wrong and should have trusted my intuition. Despite thinking everything was fine, I sent her $1,000 for a two-month rental in a nearby home.

Two days later on Monday of the following week when I expected to get a tracking number for the delivery of the keys she told me that FedEx was asking for $500. She did not have the money, and she wanted me to send her the money by Zelle so that she can send the key to me and she will pay me back by the end of the week.

2021/11/18 What is Behind the Door?

They say when a door closes another one opens. It remains true in various areas of our lives. The repetition of seeing this feels like being in a room filled with doors of various colors, making it difficult to decide which to open or avoid.

Some doors are open, concealing the unknown, while others exhibit unfamiliar complex locks. In the space between them, there is a set of keys with tags in a foreign language that I can't even read.

Should I risk it with one of the open doors? Open doors are easy, yet they are opportunities.

I approach one of the open doors and witness shadows of men and women moving about their lives in a synced motion as if they were dancing.

It was unlike a scene of peace and tranquility, but it also felt like the people were not real; their faces looked synthetic, like a projection of memories past.

It wasn't real, so I left and searched for a different door. Approaching the next door, I noticed it was closed with a lock. To the right, three keys of different materials lay beside it. Three keys of different materials, one made of glass, another made of stone, and a third made of wood, lay beside it. Which one should I use?

I chose the stone key, but it was so heavy that I dropped, and it shattered. I chose the wooden key, and I had to drop it as it smoked and as it hit the ground, it burst into flames and burned to ash. The third and last key was the glass key.

I took the glass key and, and carefully tried not to drop it and break it, the key was beautiful and was ice cold. As I looked at the key, I saw video images floating off the key as if it was a projection in front of me.

I placed the key in the lock and gently opened the door. I felt floating amidst mirrors, each a video panel to another world.

I attempted to walk through, but couldn't. A voice from the other side cautions, "You are not ready," while another asserts, "You are not welcome." As I feel a hand press against my chest, I choose to leave the room, only to find the door vanished before me.

I took a step back about fifty feet to see all the doors and suddenly a neon sign pointed me to a red door. I was not sure, red usually means danger but then again all I could do is trust the sign. I approached the door, but it was also locked.

Three locks, three keys made of rusted metal, different colors - blue, green, yellow. But which key fits which lock? Another puzzle before I could enter. I matched each lock with a key and opened the door to reveal a world unlike anything I'd ever seen, a beautiful world of adventure.

2021/11/20 New Friends

For the past two days, I have been busy making new friends. After my last attempt at securing a new place to live failed, turning into someone defrauding me out of $1,000.

Spare Room app helped me find an affordable place, but I have to share a bathroom. I'll have my own room, and three new companions. Texting Jasmine for the past two days, we've discovered surprising similarities between us. One occupies one out of three bedrooms, and I'll be occupying the third bedroom.

The couple is one from the Dominican Republic and the other from Puerto Rico while the third woman I don't yet know, but I'm about to find out very soon.

Texting with Jasmine, I discovered that her partner shares my love for technology and Sci-Fi. We also realized that she is a nurse, and we have many other shared interests.

After thirty minutes of texting, I felt it was the right time to ask if we could meet, given our common interests. I believe our bond will work as I live with three women who will support my journey as a transgender woman.

2021/11/20 One Step at a Time

Ever since I came out as transgender and changed my name to Tamara, I've been taking steps to move forward by telling my employer, family, and friends.

I have gradually gained new friends and lost others, because of personal views or religious principles. It has been challenging, but it has strengthened me and made me more determined.

Today I met with my niece Jessie for lunch and had a great time with her. Lunch was quick, but the conversation was rewarding, and I enjoyed my time with her.

Later I went to Arbor Place Mall to pierce once more my right ear and after that, I drove back home to see my son and his girlfriend, Stephanie.

2021/11/21 What Am I Supposed to Do?

Today, I'll visit Jasmine and check out the room where I'll be able to openly embrace living as Tamara. I'm excited about having some alone time for the first time in thirty years. Despite that, I'll remain connected to my children and ex-wife as friends.

December 1 will be here in one more week after Thanksgiving, which is this upcoming Thursday, and I'm already prepared and my luggage ready for the move.

2021/11/24 The Search for a New Place

My recent days have been filled with excitement. My son's girlfriend, Tamara, met me for the first time on Sunday. It went well, and I expressed my happiness and appreciation for her presence. I was afraid she will leave my son over my transition, but she truly loves him.

On Monday I had a man named Omar respond to my message on the Roomster app. I've searched for a new rental home for three weeks and messaged multiple people about renting a room with a private bathroom. He's the only one who responded, so I'll meet him on the Saturday after Thanksgiving.

I discovered Sephora provides makeup services for transgender women. I opted for a ninety-minute full makeover and scheduled my appointment for Saturday at 1:00 p.m. I'm really looking forward to a more beautiful version of myself.

Today after work, I'll visit a nail salon to mend a broken nail and get a professional manicure for Thanksgiving.

2021/11/30 Looking Ahead

Tomorrow is December first and I have some important events this month. Besides Christmas and New Year's, I have a virtual consultation on the twentieth with the Facial Team for facial feminization surgery evaluation. On December 30, I have a court date in Cobb County to legally change my name to Tamara Rivera, this is certainly a very exciting month and I'm looking ahead to a new me in 2022.

2021/12/03 Excitement is Waiting

I haven't been writing in my diary every day like I used to, not because there's nothing exciting happening. I can't keep up with my fast-paced life.

I prioritize my appearance as Tamara, taking time to select my outfits. I change my wardrobe multiple times before going out and do my nails.

I create unique nail art styles and receive compliments. My hair is the one thing that I can't decide how to style. I'm never satisfied with my hair and settle for whatever style works.

Since I struggle with makeup, I choose to go makeup-free and wear a mask in light of the ongoing pandemic. I have a significant learning curve in this area.

2021/12/05 Dreams on Hold

My life has been a constant struggle. Despite my ambition, I can't progress as much as I want, which saddens me.

I could not complete high school because of being forced to quit before my last semester. My father's imprisonment and refusal to support us forced me to leave school and take a low-paying job to help my mom with my younger siblings.

I've always struggled for higher education, but lack of a high school diploma hasn't held me back in certain areas.

I have a successful job with a company that requires a degree in IT. I would love to take a course in cosmetology, so I went to Empire Beauty School, but before I can get in, I need to have a high school diploma, so here is where my dreams are on hold. Does the absence of a high school diploma hinder my dreams?

2021/12/07 Shopping for Shoes

Last Sunday, I went shoe shopping. I have been wearing my blue suede booties for a while and I'm starting to feel like I need a variety of shoes. I visited the DSW store in Lenox, but I only found cute shoes and not the black pumps and booties I was looking for.

I went through the women's shoe aisles and spotted several adorable shoes. Women's shoes offer many options, but size 11 is harder to find. There is only one size 12 shoe I came across. I couldn't find black booties in my size, so I settled for gray size 11.

I spent over an hour there for one pair of shoes. I purchased the gray booties for $70.00 at DSW Shoes and headed home. I had second thoughts about the shoe purchase while driving. I used to easily buy shoes, but now the shopping experience has changed.

My focus is on style, color, and fit. The experience was enthralling, and thoughts of the shoes I purchased raced through my mind as I drove home. After I got home, I browsed the DSW Shoes website for more shoes and instead of one, I ended up buying a pair of black pumps and a pair of chunky heel boots in black. I have to wait up to seven days for my new shoes to arrive.

2021/12/09 The Day After

I took the COVID-19 vaccine in May or April 2021 and waited a while for the booster shot. I'm experiencing mild flu symptoms one day later. Yesterday, I experienced body aches, chills, and a runny nose.

2021/12/10 Mind Your Pronouns!

I took Thursday off because of mild flu symptoms, but felt well enough by noon to run errands.

I dressed in baggy, multicolor boho pants, a blue tunic with lace shoulders, and a long pink sweater. I also wore light makeup to cover my beard shadow and accessorized with flowery sunglasses and a light Michael Kors perfume.

I felt good until I went to pick up my prescriptions at Walgreens. This was a low point for me. I often visit this place for my prescriptions. I typically have positive experiences shopping for beauty products, with employees using my preferred pronouns respectfully.

I waited in line behind two other customers for prescriptions. My time to step up finally came and the first words of the young woman behind the counter were "How can I help you, sir?" I initially wanted to reprimand her, but I diverted the discussion to my pending prescriptions. They weren't ready and said they'd be available later, addressing me as sir despite my appearance.

She used male pronouns without considering my feelings, which I found disrespectful. I walked out feeling humiliated and all I wanted was to speak up and talk to a manager, but I went on about my business.

On my way to Cumberland Mall, I returned the gray booties I purchased at DSW Shoes, but I was hungry and headed to Del Taco in Smyrna, Georgia, and ordered a plate of smothered taquitos.

My experience was flawless, except for being mis gendered when ordering my drink. I felt a sinking feeling that I was missing something. Am I not dressed femininely enough? What's causing the sudden lack of respect? Is today a national disrespect day?

I sobbed in the dining room while eating, feeling humiliated and speechless. Instead of going home, I went to the mall. I arrived at DSW Shoes and returned my gray booties, and after that made the best of my day.

2021/12/11 Breakfast comes first,

I had no plans for today. I started my day off with a blank slate, but things changed quickly as the day developed. After breakfast, I went to get my car from my son's shop. He borrowed my car yesterday while his was being repaired, then drove his car to his girlfriend's house. Today, he drove me there to retrieve my car.

On my way home, I drove to Walgreens' pharmacy to refill my estradiol prescription, even though I had refilled it just three days ago. When I opened the bottle at home, I discovered the pills had been crushed into powder, with about 90 percent of them affected. After the pharmacist gave me a fresh bottle, I headed back home.

Christmas decorations are next, and we only have fourteen days left to put them out. My daughter arrived in the afternoon, and after setting up a few decorations, we watched a movie on Amazon Prime. Reality hit me when my daughter left after the movie. I'll be moving on January 1, 2022. Despite the short distance, I'll feel emotionally distant from my dear children.

2021/12/12 Staying True to Yourself

Many wake up without purpose, except the innate goal to survive. That's an amazing gift we share.

Michele Obama captured the essence of staying true to oneself. "Stay true to yourself and never let what somebody says distract you from your goals."

Embracing my identity as a transgender woman, I quickly found my true self and am eager for further personal development in 2022.

2021/12/15 Rejection Hurts

Despite feeling better about myself and being loved and accepted, the hurtful words of my brother still linger in my mind. Hearing it from him was the worst experience. I felt pain, humiliation, and rejection. Memories overwhelmed me while I worked last Tuesday, and I cried.

The chats with my aunt Titi in New York bring me love. I have been chatting with her on Facebook and she makes me feel good and loved. She sends me loving and hopeful messages.

2021/12/16 Opening the Virtual Bandages

I expect an exciting day today. After work, I have an orientation with the Facial Team to preview my post-surgery appearance. My appointment got rescheduled to today, Thursday, December 16, giving me a chance to uncover what's hidden behind the virtual bandages.

This is the moment I've been waiting for to see myself as a woman and gain confidence and I am also considering voice feminization surgery. I am eager about voice feminization surgery to sound more feminine in person and on the phone. People use pronouns based on your voice over the phone. That's human nature. I don't blame anyone.

2021/12/17 "Me acostumbre a" (Spanish version)

"Me acostumbre a ocupar toda la cama al dormir, a no cocinar los domingos y a volver a mi casa a la hora que me da la gana.

Me acostumbre a, no dar explicaciones y hacer lo que me gusta sin que nadie me critique.

Me acostumbre a comer a la media noche y a ver mis programas favoritos, a cantar en voz alta y bailar por toda la casa.

Me acostumbre a recibir llamadas a cada rato y contestar mensajes muy tarde, a salir con mis amigas y viajar uno que otro fin de semana.

Me acostumbre al olor del café por las mañanas y a caminar descalza por el jardín, a tardar cuando me toca arreglarme y a cancelar citas al último momento

¿Sabes porque me acostumbre a mí?

¿A mis cosas, a mi vida y a estar sola?

Porque es simplemente maravilloso estar a solas conmigo misma"

(Autor desconocido).

(English translation) "I got used to"

"I got used to occupying the entire bed when I sleep, not cooking on Sundays, and coming back home whenever I want.

I got used to not giving explanations and doing what I like without anyone criticizing me.

I got used to eating at midnight and watching my favorite shows, singing out loud, and dancing all over the house.

I got used to receiving calls all the time and answering messages very late, going out with my friends, and traveling every other weekend.

I got used to the smell of coffee in the morning and walking barefoot through the garden, late when I have to get ready and to cancel appointments at the last moment

Do you know why I got used to it?

To my things, to my life and to be alone?

Because it's just wonderful to be alone with myself."

(Unknown author)

2021/12/18 Facial Feminization

On Thursday, I had a virtual consultation with Dr. Gutierrez from Spain, where the Facial Team's offices are. It was earlier than expected. Lucky it came in about five minutes prior to my lunch break from work. The meeting was forty minutes long and I was delighted with the Spanish doctor.

He had a light complexion, dark hair, and a captivating smile, a calm demeanor, and soft voice. He explained the necessary changes for a more feminine appearance.

2021/12/19 Artistic Expressions

Nail art has fascinated me since I started doing my own nails. I have created 12 unique styles that I have been placing online on Facebook and Instagram and I have received compliments on my latest designs. It took me three hours to create a complex Christmas nail design with vibrant colors and glitter.

2021/12/20. It feels Wonderful!

When I wake up at 5 am, the first thing on my mind is my daily exercise routine. I start by checking my blood pressure, which is usually below normal. Then, I turn on the news and begin my workout. I typically exercise for 30 to 45 minutes and follow it up with a 45-minute run on my stepper machine. This routine has been instrumental in keeping me fit and energized in the morning.

2021/12/21 Broken Silence

Since coming out as a transgender woman two months ago, many wonderful things have occurred. I experienced painful moments because of family rejection. My world felt like it had crumbled, leaving me isolated. My only connections are my sister in Florida, my niece in Georgia, and my aunt in New York, whom I communicate with on Facebook.

Finally, my youngest sister Linda called me last night after silence from my family. It served as a brief icebreaker. I was not expecting this call. I wasn't hopeful when others said they will call. My aunt told my sister in Florida that it's time to break the ice and start anew with our family.

2021/12/21 Disappointing Results

I wanted a facial treatment to reduce fine lines and improve my skin's appearance. After careful research, I decided on a product from Perricone MD comprising four products for day and night. The daytime and nighttime regimen included the use of four products.

The daytime regimen.

1. Cold Plasma MD
2. High Potency Amine Face Lift
3. Face Finishing & Firming Moisturizer
4. Firming Eye Lift

The nighttime regimen.

1. Cold Plasma MD
2. High Potency Evening Repair
3. Face Finishing & Firming Moisturizer
4. Firming Eye Lift

I followed instructions precisely, and everything went well for two weeks. I saw changes in my face, fine lines reduced, my skin felt softer, and my eyes looked brighter.

I was happy with the results, but in my third week I felt like my skin was burning, and one morning I woke up to see my face full of red blotches. My face blazed and my skin seemed to tear apart.

I never expected this, and my world crumbled. How can I confront the world in this condition?

I never realized I had sensitive skin and now I must find out how to get my skin back in shape. Coconut oil, as suggested by my wife, improved my skin and reduced the redness.

2021/12/22 Long Distance Friends

In a world rapidly growing smaller technologically speaking since the internet has given us communication at the speed of light, you put anything online, and in a matter of seconds, it's news across the country and the world.

When I came out as a transgender and posted a video with my story on my company's transgender resources group. On that day, I got a surprising message from a woman named Katherine who works at Cox Automotive in California. Her message was heartwarming.

Ever since we have become pen-pals. I sent her a Christmas card a month ago and got a beautiful bracelet in return. It has pink, baby blue, and white beads on one side with white tiles that spell out Tamara, and a silver dragonfly on the other side.

It brought tears of joy to my heart that a stranger I have not even met put so much thought into something lovely and heartwarming along with a handwritten note on lavender paper that said the meaning of the colors and the dragonfly and this is what she wrote.

> December 14, 2021 Thank you for the beautiful Christmas card, I'm so happy to hear that you will officially be welcoming the new year as Tamara. I made you this bracelet to celebrate your journey. The dragonfly symbolizes change, transformation, adaptability, and self-realization. Wishing you all that and more in the new year.
>
> Celebrating you,
>
> Katherine 2021/12/23 Request Granted

Two weeks ago, I asked Cox for time off on December 30 and my request was denied, this made me cry since this is a very important date for me. This date will start off 2022 for me as Tamara, I have been expecting this since November 11, 2021, the date I went to the Cobb County Court to file a petition for a name change.

I talked to my company's management about the denial of time off and was advised to speak to the general manager. I was nervous and felt afraid to talk to him since he seems hard to talk to and was sure he was going to say no, which I was not ready to hear, but also I didn't want to risk my job.

But I did not want to miss this court date either since this is an important step in my transition.

Yesterday afternoon I sent the general manager a message through Teams asking him to reconsider my request and shared with him by email the two-page petition for my name change, to my surprise he was understanding and sympathetic to my request and granted me the time.

2021/12/25 Christmas Joy

Today is Christmas, the most amazing and beautiful holiday of the year, a time for family and friends, a time to share a meal a smile, and of course presents.

This Christmas is certainly a very special one I'm sure my kids and wife had a hard time choosing a present for me since my transition. I've had some tense moments and some good times, but this was a very special day for us all.

I gave my wife a shared present: a brand-new Dell laptop, with contributions from the kids and me. All her previous laptops were hand-me-downs until the last one, a used laptop I bought for $100 from my daughter's friend Jazmine, which quickly experienced a catastrophic hard drive failure.

We gave her a new laptop a month earlier for wrapping. Surprisingly, we all received great gifts. I received a flannel blanket, an Amazon Echo speaker, a JBL Bluetooth speaker, and a surprise gift from my wife.

A week before Christmas, she asked me about my desired gifts, a yearly tradition ensuring we receive what we want. Despite my initial reluctance, I requested earrings and she surprised me with a white frame LED makeup mirror.

I received an unexpected call from my eldest sister on Christmas day. Though short, it was sweet and made me happy. Christmas brings a lot of joy and happiness, and this Christmas was special indeed.

2021/12/26 Year In Review?

I'm not ready for this moment. Despite having an interesting year, I still have five days left. In the next five days, I have two important dates on my calendar: December 30, my legal name change to Tamara, and December 31, New Year's Eve.

2021/12/28 Three More Days 2021 has been a tough year for everyone, but despite the troubles, plus a virus that continues to develop into other variants. Despite this, I believe in continuing my forward momentum to my M2F transition this has been a struggle, which may never be over but only faith and determination keeps me going.

Only three days left in 2021, and I feel mounting anxiety as I approach my final milestone. On December 30, I have a court date for a hearing on my name change to close to 2021 and start 2022 as Tamara Rivera turning a new chapter in my life.

2021/12/29 What's On for Today?

Besides working and meeting my new landlord, Miranda, I have no plans for the day. I am open to accepting whatever comes my way and will adjust my plans accordingly. Plans often fail because of unforeseen circumstances, especially in 2021. The ongoing COVID-19 pandemic has made it difficult to stick to schedules due to the disruptions it has caused.

2021/12/30 Year One

This year has certainly been a challenge with COVID-19 claiming more lives with it and the economy tight. In 2021, new technologies, space missions, and electric cars were exciting. The most exciting thing for me was coming out as transgender. It was always in my heart for a long time. I wonder why I didn't do it earlier in my youth.

It was in October that I took the bold steps to not only go to an LGBT specialist; I began HRT hormone treatment and later filed a petition for a name change on November 10. This was the one thing I planned.

I would have given myself more time, they scheduled the hearing for December 30 at 9:30 a.m. The court date arrived, and I was anxious not knowing what to expect. Surprisingly, the judge granted my name change to Tamara Rivera.

Hearing those words, I went straight to Waffle House for breakfast, speechless and in disbelief. Tears streamed down my face as I ate and drank coffee. I was ecstatic and couldn't control my emotions.

2021/12/31 The Future Is Waiting

Today marks the end of 2021, leaving behind my former self and its history of hardship. The future holds a promising year ahead for Tamara Rivera. I'm taking my remaining men's clothing to a consignment shop and close the doors to a life that was.

2021/12/31 Before my Transition

I've written extensively about my transition process, but haven't written much about my life before transitioning.

From the moment I recognized my discomfort with myself, confusion and questions flooded in. Am I gay? Am I supposed to be a woman? I never felt like a man. I lived a life of pretense and constant dissatisfaction with myself.

An adopted uncle raped at nine me and realized I liked it. He spread the word that I was gay, but I played along. Since then, I had intimate encounters with young boys in my neighborhood. I believed my fate as a gay individual was sealed, but I knew it was more complex than that.

Wearing women's clothing doesn't determine one's sexual orientation. I took an interest in lingerie early on. At ten years old, I stole panties from my family and kept them in a shoe box. My mom found them, cried, chastised me, and prayed, but I would do it again.

When I started puberty, I grew body hair on my legs and chest and I felt so ashamed of my body. Growing up, my intense feelings made me realize there was more to me than just being gay. Amid confusion, an unexpected source opened my eyes.

I saw pornography at my neighbor's house, featuring the most beautiful trans women. Because of lack of familiarity, they called them chicks with dicks. I realized life goes beyond being male or female. I wasn't aware of another gender, but it seems like where I belong.

2022/01/01 Happy New Year

I am excited to start my first day of the new year as Tamara Rivera. I slept at 1:00 a.m. and I woke up groggy from last night's champagne celebration with family.

For my first full day of 2022, I went to a nail salon. I went to Regal Nails at Walmart, but they were closed. I proceeded to Ulta Beauty, where I discovered the adjacent nail salon was closed as well. Most places are closed since it's January 1st, and I was convinced that others were closed as well.

I went inside Ulta Beauty and picked up cuticle oil and a gold flakes enamel and as I was ready to leave, I mentioned to a young woman at the store that I was looking for a nail salon but all places I considered are closed.

She spun around and gestured across the parking lot to a line of single-story shops, pointing out an Xfinity store, and mentioned a new nail salon named Allure Nails and Spa.

I bought nail polish and cuticle oil, then went to Allure Nails and Spa. I walked into the salon through the glass door, and I noticed a young man doing a woman's nails.

He asked me what I wanted to have done, and after showing him my nails and explaining to him what I wanted, he went on with his work without a single word. I stood there for a second as I looked at the large room where women were getting a manicure while others were getting a pedicure and others a massage.

I looked around I noticed a counter with a tablet that had a message to sign in to register. I typed in my name, phone number, and date of birth, and I saw a row of chairs behind me where a young woman was waiting for her turn.

The chairs looked more like for children since they were low to the ground and as I sat down, I felt like I was seven feet tall with knees above my hips as I sat there and waited for a young man that was doing a woman's nails walked over and asked me what I wanted.

I sat waiting for about ten minutes when he finally called me and the first thing that he asked me was to wash my hands, but I needed to use the restroom after that, I returned to him and sat down on a chair facing the young man that was about to do my nails.

He started by cleaning my nails to remove the nail polish. With a delicate touch, he used an e-file to remove the gold flake lines from my nails and then polished them with a buffer.

He cleaned my nails and applied a clear base coat to my left hand. Then, he asked me to put my hand under the UV lamp. Next, he repeated the process on my right hand.

After applying the base coat, he then applied the gel coat and later a lavender, pink gel color he had previously chosen. He also did an interesting leaf artwork on one nail in each hand and finally applied the top coat.

I checked the time before he started and it took an hour from start to finish. This exceeded my expectations in terms of cost at $57, but the result and the experience justified the expense.

2022/01/02 Moving Day 1

I have been working my way to this point for a few weeks and the time is now. However. it has been the hardest decision. I lived with my spouse for nearly thirty years and twenty-two years at our current home with our two children.

My son, now twenty-five, had moved out to go to an automotive tech school in Orlando, Florida where he lived for two years before returning home. And later my daughter also moved out to a shared apartment with high school friends and after one year, she is returning home to help her mom after I move out.

Moving fifteen minutes away from home after years of sharing walls with an amazing family has left me heartbroken. Though I will miss being with them, I'm not far away from home in case they need me.

2022/01/03 Mood Swings!

I woke up feeling good today, despite feeling a bit sleepy. I worked on the first Monday of the new year. I completed my morning routine, had breakfast and coffee, and began working at 8:00 a.m.

As I stood up in front of my computer, I felt a sudden sense of sadness, an urge to cry for no apparent reason. Despite obstacles, my life is going well. On New Year's Eve, my family called to wish me a happy New Year, and my brother, who hasn't spoken to me since coming out, sent me a text saying "happy New Year, bro. I'm happy and have much to celebrate.

Why was I sad on this first Monday of the new year? I felt a deepening sadness and a compelling need to cry. Lunchtime came around and I had already had my lunch since I work from home. At about 11:45 I ran from my office room to the kitchen and placed my lunch in the microwave for 1 minute and 30 seconds.

I had my lunch as I waited for the clock to reach the 12:00 mark so that I could clock out. After clocking out, my purpose became clear.

I went to my bedroom where the family cat was there, lying on my bed. I fell onto my bed, face-first on the pillow, and unleashed my anxiety. I fell asleep to the gentle purring of my cat while tears streamed down my face.

I slept for 40 minutes. I woke up feeling better and ready to finish my first workday. It was only a mood swing. Crying and sleeping helped me through it.

2022/01/07 Final Moving Day Approaching

Today is my last full day at the place I made my home for the last twenty-five years. The only thing left is to move my office desk, computer, and bed. Tomorrow, I start a new life as Tamara Rivera in a new place, representing a new chapter. What are the challenges that lie ahead?

Unsure, but prepared to face this confidently and proud of my achievements. It's the toughest decision I've made, but necessary for progress.

2022/01/09 Moving Completed

I finished moving and starting a new chapter. Only my bed, office desk, and a few minor items remained to be moved. I reserved a van from U-HAUL yesterday to pick it up today from a small store in Dallas.

I arrived thirty minutes late and walked in. I was greeted by a young male who appeared to be friendly. He looked like he was Middle Eastern perhaps from Pakistan and after I showed him the reservation number from my phone he asked for my driver's license.

He checked the picture and questioned if I had my driver's license. Neither he nor the older gentleman with him believed that the person in the ID was the same woman standing before them.

I confirmed my identity to him. Processing the order took 20 minutes because of a canceled reservation. Both men treated me with respect, addressing me as madam, and I felt delighted.

I quickly picked up the U-HAUL van with my son's help. I loaded the van in Powder Springs and drove to Dallas, Georgia. I unloaded the van and returned it. Then, I drove my son home and went back to Dallas, stopping by Walmart for groceries.

2022/01/11 It's Freezing

I recently moved into a shared home, where I have been occupying a bedroom with a private bathroom for the past three days. Everything was going well until last night when the temperature suddenly dropped to 30°.

Unfortunately, this is when the heater decided to stop working, leaving the entire house freezing cold.

2022/01/13 On A High Note

The year 2022 is off to a good start for me. I have new female supportive friends and new exciting moments coming up. I am looking forward to a fun-filled day next Sunday.

I have a lunch date at 1:00 p.m. with my new friend Amara, the first girls' day out since COVID.

I have a nail salon appointment with Dafney after lunch. She has been a longtime friend and good moral support for me. This depends on the weather, with temperatures in the mid-30s and the possibility of snow.

2022/01/17 Where's the Snow?

Atlanta has had several days of low 30° temperatures and is expected to receive snow. Snow is a rare event in the Southern states, making even an inch a big deal.

It's the second weekend of 2022 and we're expecting snow for the first time since Jan 2020, causing empty shelves at local Walmart stores for bread, milk, and water.

I moved to Dallas, Georgia a week earlier and came to my home in Powder Springs to be with my children during the pending snow. Despite heavy snowfall, it didn't stick due to prior rain, leaving only ice the next morning.

2022/01/19 Sick Day

Yesterday started as usual, get up early and after listening to the morning news and having breakfast, I sat at my desk, powered up my work computer and started promptly at 8:00 a.m. but something felt wrong. I had no energy and rapidly felt worse by the minute. Body aches, fever and a headache and cough, I thought that I could stay and work at least till noon but before 10:00 a.m. I threw in the towel and told my employer that I'm leaving work early since I was sick.

I promptly went to bed after logging off work. I slept around six hours intermittently. Later, I went back to sleep at 8:00 p.m. and slept through the night. Although I woke up a few times, I shivered as I got up and returned to bed. I woke up at 6:00 a.m. finally. After nearly twenty hours of sleep, I felt significantly better. My body needed that rest.

I called my employer in the morning and excused myself for the day so that I could rest. I did not exactly stay home, since I legally changed my name on December 30, 2021. I now have evidence of my legal status as Tamara Rivera.

2022/01/21 Devine Inspiration

As humans, we find ourselves in a constant battle, trying to unravel the enigmatic intricacies of our Lord's grand design. Inside my mind, I feel an intense struggle as I grapple with unseen forces, like a tempestuous storm raging within. Yet, amidst this inner turmoil, one truth shines through with dazzling clarity - my gender change does not alter the boundless love our Creator has for me. Like a delicate thread, I remain intricately connected to the divine, a sensation that caresses my very soul.

2022/01/22 Separation Anxiety

It's been about two weeks since I moved out of the home, I shared for nearly twenty-five years with my family and though my wife and I had not had a physical relationship for several years we still have a good friendship and remain close.

The move was a personal choice, adjusting to a new life alone after thirty years. Moments of solitude arise since the pandemic struck two years ago. I worked from home while everyone else was away until 7:00 p.m.

My biggest concern after work was making a tasty meal everyone enjoys. Some days I had meals pre-planned, while others I searched frantically for inspiration.

Wednesdays are for leftovers, and Fridays are for pizza or takeout. Weekend breakfasts were my specialty, filled with scrambled eggs, sausage, mushrooms, onions, garlic, and herbs.

Cooking used to bring me joy, especially when I shared it with my family. Now, it's difficult to cook breakfast for just myself, like I did this morning. I felt an uncomfortable sensation that I have no one else to share my meal with and see them enjoying it. This brought me to tears, and I sobbed for a few minutes as I take a bite. It felt like I have lost the sense of worth through my cooking.

2022/01/23 Time for My Children

I started my day with a pre-planned schedule. First thing this morning I had an appointment with my son to go to Gainesville, Georgia with him so that he can check out a small Nissan truck that he's planning on buying, after a quick breakfast and a cup of coffee we headed out in his 2009 VW Rabbit.

I taught both my kids to drive. My daughter learned on a 2008 Chevrolet HHR, which I gave her after she got her license. My son learned to drive a 2012 Fiat 500 POP with a five-speed manual transmission.

After passing his test, we went to a dealership to buy his first car, a 2006 Nissan 350 Z. He's a fan of these cars because I own a classic 1977 280 Z, the generation before the 1978 280 ZX. Now he's into the famous Nissan sports car.

He attended a mechanic school in Florida for Nissan automotive technology, while my daughter pursued arts and animation.

2022/01/26 Sharing a Meal

Cooking brings me joy, especially when I can share a meal with others. Yesterday was the first time since I moved to where I am now that I was able to prepare a meal. I bought a pita kit from Walmart with three flat bread, meat, and sauce.

I heated the pita bread on a tray, warmed up the cooked meat, and sauteed mushrooms, onions, and garlic in butter. After I finished preparing everything, I started assembling it all. First, I spread the white sauce on the bread, then delicately placed the meat with toppings of onions, mushrooms, and garlic. The food had such an appealing appearance; it looked absolutely delicious.

I took the first bite of one as I carefully picked it up and it tasted so satisfying that I wanted to share it with one of my roommates. I placed one on a plate and walked up to her room.

I knocked on her closed bedroom door and she allowed me to enter. I offered her the plate, but she declined due to the beef. She doesn't eat beef or pork. I walked downstairs to the kitchen and cried. I miss the ability to create meals that can be enjoyed by everyone.

2022/02/03 Don't Call Me Sir

I rarely write in my journal, but today something good happened that made my day sweet. I had a doctor's appointment at 8:40 a.m. today. I consulted with my doctor after the nurse took my blood work and blood pressure, which was 128/80.

My doctor came in about five minutes later and I talked to him about my progress with hormones. My body is changing, with my breasts, hips, and butt getting bigger.

I miss my family when I go shopping or eat. I cry for not having them around to share a meal with, but I need to work on it.

After I left the doctor's office I went to the Social Security Administration office in Villa Rica, Georgia the office was closed but there was a security officer at the door for those who had an appointment. since I did not have an appointment I couldn't go in, but he was nice and he gave me a form to fill out and advised me to call to set up an appointment.

On my way back home I stopped by the drive-through at McDonald's and placed my order, and the man taking my order addressed me as sir twice, to which I insisted, "Don't call me Sir." I could hear his voice murmur, "I'm sorry mam." I drove around to the first window to pay. The young man with a big smile apologized once more saying, I am sorry mam.

2022/02/08 Dating My Girlfriends

The past few days have been amazing. Every day I am having new experiences and I am happier than ever before. My life as Tamara is developing and growing. I'm meeting new people, making new friends online on Facebook and Instagram.

My popularity is increasing despite having few followers. My top highlights of the week were two dinner dates. Last Friday, I had a great night with my friend Charise at Ruby Tuesdays.

We stayed for two hours and formed a deep connection. We discussed our friendship, reminisced about work, and then she inquired about my coming out.

She asked if I made this decision overnight, but I reassured her that it was the result of a lifetime of suffering. I finally took a stand and came out as transgender, feeling liberated.

2022/02/12 Amazing Day

Today I worked four hours in the morning from 6:30 a.m. to 10:30 a.m. and later was the big day that my friend Amara and I planned on for a week, a day that till it happened, I feared would not happen. Since transitioning, I've had several disappointments that hurt me deeply and I was beginning to lose faith in people.

When I got up this morning, I had already dressed and nearly prepared to go, so all I needed was makeup. After I got off work, I headed to my bathroom to get my face ready for makeup.

This is a long process for me since I take about an hour to prepare my skin with a moisturizer, then apply the foundation, followed by lashes and eyebrows, and my lips. The more I practice, the better I become.

We kept in contact through the day, building excitement to the first part of our day, and after several calls, we finally met at the Publix store in Smyrna, Georgia on the corner of the EW Connector and South Cobb Dr. Our plan was to buy a sandwich since we would not have time to sit down for lunch. While on her way to Smyrna, Amara enjoyed the music playing on the radio. I called her and asked what she likes on a sandwich and we both agreed on tuna with lettuce and tomato and mayo and mustard on wheat bread.

In front of me, there were four people in line. I wore a stylish black blouse with red roses printed on it and black pants that draped around my legs and opened as I walked, revealing my legs dancing with the wind.

I had applied foundation to my legs to cover some scars and make my skin look even toned and appear as if I had stockings and wore dark blue boots and had a red clutch bag in my hands.

I approached the counter, where a masked woman took my order for a roasted tuna sandwich. She had to go slice it. She came back and as she prepared my sandwich, she acknowledged my sweet Jazmine perfume saying that I smell good.

Upon getting the sandwich from the Publix deli, Amara had already arrived. Our first stop, The Fox Theater, hosted an awe-inspiring performance by Alvin. It was a truly beautiful and unforgettable moment for both of us, as it was our first time there. In Georgia for forty years, never visited theater. Expensive, but worth it.

After the Fox Theater, we walked back to the parking deck which was also an adventure. We spotted a young street performer playing the trumpet. Amara took a picture, and we kept walking. Later, we stopped at a club where people were enjoying music and drinks.

They were not taking more guests, but Amara talked to the young woman standing outside and she allowed us to walk in. After taking photos, we returned to the car and headed home. We went to Publix to pick up my Silver Hyundai Veloster. Then we stopped at the racetrack nearby to get gas before heading to my rental home in Dallas, Georgia. We had an exhilarating day full of adventure, and now it was time to eat dinner.

I informed Amara days ago that I planned to make salmon with wild rice and veggies. When we got home, I parked in the garage and she parked behind me in the driveway. Then we headed to the kitchen.

In the kitchen, I gathered the ingredients and started cooking. I cooked the wild rice for about fourty five minutes, since it takes the longest. I placed the salmon on the grill and cook the vegetables as Amara prepared the salad.

We both worked together to prepare the meal - I cooked while she washed dishes, prepared the salad, and we enjoyed the music. The salmon came with butter and pesto, to which I added chopped rosemary.

I cooked it well and then placed the salmon, rice, and vegetables on the plate and avocado on the side. The plate looked beautiful, and we both took pictures with our phones before we sat to eat and savor the meal. The dish was incredibly delicious, and we enjoyed it with a sweet rose wine. Valentine's Day was beautiful and amazing.

2022/02/16 Three Amigas

Valentine's Day came, but it has not stopped its heartwarming energy. Since February 14, I've had interesting days with my two closest friends, Amara and Reina. Our friendship has grown stronger, and we are always in touch like best friends, even though we haven't known each other for long. Since transitioning,

I have lost a lot of friends, but none that I miss now. The special friendship I now have with Amara and Reina means so much more to me than lost friends.

This upcoming weekend I'm having breakfast with Reina while Amara is going to travel to San Francisco for the weekend for personal business.

A true friend is loyal, honest, respectful, supportive, and comforting. True friends boost your self-esteem and remain loyal no matter what changes you go through in life, if you transition and they are there for you, those are the friends you should stay with, if they walk away, let them vanish inti the sunset.

2022/02/17 Self-Care is Love

I love taking care of my nails and creating beautiful designs, fingernails are like an artist's canvas and a good assortment of nail polish is the artist's palette full of color. There are files, buffers, and tools to shape and prepare your nails. Beautiful nail art reflects your dedication and passion.

2022/02/19 Lady's Time

Today I had a lot of fun… no, I didn't go to a park, a movie theater, or a restaurant to eat. I went to Stone Mountain, Georgia to visit my friend Reina at her home and Amara met us there about an hour and a half later. We were there to have homemade Colombian arepas for a late breakfast.

Reina serves fresh arepas with various toppings in separate bowls. After eating, we spent the day chatting in the living room. Yet another first experience on Women's Day. I've been here with women before, feeling a sense of belonging, but never this relaxed.

2022/02/20 A Beautiful and Captivating Smile

I have a beautiful memory from yesterday. Before I headed to Reina's home, I stopped by the cleaners to pick up a top I had to alter by shortening the sleeves. As I walked from my car to the cleaners, a nice light-skinned gentleman with a big beautiful smile saw me and he stood there at the door and held it open for me.

He was not that good-looking, but something about his beautiful smile is captivating and he continued to smile as he held the door for me to walk into the cleaners.

He walked in behind me and he stood a few steps away from me as he looked at me with that smile. I got my top and was happy with the work the cleaners did with the short sleeves and I said out loud that it looked gorgeous and he quietly replied with a smile, "It sure is."

As I turned around to walk to my car, I looked at him and waved my hand, showing my nail art, and said bye to him as he stood there still smiling, and I walked away with that smile in my mind.

This morning, I still remember his smile. I never imagined I could make a man smile so radiantly. Leaving the cleaners, I carried on, but the man's captivating smile remained with me throughout the day.

2022/02/27 The Adventures Continue

Earlier this week I logged in to the Social Security website to access my account and see the progress of my name change and I was happy that it now shows my name as Tamara Rivera. I was happy to see this, now the long process of changing my name on all my documents and creditors begins, my time to bring Tamera full circle and erase my formal name from history.

The first place I changed my name was my bank Wells Fargo. I felt great as I entered the bank. There was a nice-looking young man dressed in a black vest. I could tell that he works there as he held the door open for me and greeted me.

I entered first, with two men behind. I was the first in line at the recently opened bank. The bank teller called me to the counter and after explaining the reason for my visit she pointed to a waiting area to take a seat she said one of the banking associates can help me with that.

I walked to the waiting area and before I could sit down, the same young man at the door walked up to me and asked me what I needed.

I informed him of my name change and the need to update my account. He requested legal documents, so I presented the state-stamped letter and Social Security office envelope. He clarified that the state letter was sufficient.

He asked me to wait in his office as he walked past me. He appeared to have a light skin tone, and even with a black mask, I could see that he was smiling. I can only imagine his smile, clutching my state letter.

2022/06/21 Crying Journal 9:00 a.m. today. I had an unexplained urge to cry, but I kept pushing forward. Once, she suffered chains, abuse, and despair. It tore her apart like a house battered by a storm. "Blessed is the woman who has broken the chains to live FREE and thrive."

2022/06/26 Time To Serve God

I avoided church for years due to fear of pressure to repent for my sins and revert to my insecure self, always hiding behind walls.

Today for the last nine months, I have been living as Tamara and I'm happy I searched online to find a church where I can serve the Lord without anyone accusing or pointing their accusatory fingers at me for being a transgender woman.

I found a church where I can serve God and be among like-minded people. I've been going to Pilgrimage Presbyterian Church for five weeks and have met kind and respectful people.

2022/06/29 Another Heartbreak

Today I got up as usual, but I was procrastinating and thought about taking a break from exercise since I felt a bit tired. It was not till 9:00 a.m. that I walked out the door and began my morning walk. It was nearly thirty minutes later that Amara called me.

She was mad because she believed I betrayed her trust by messaging her family on Facebook. She even sent me a screenshot, asking me to unfriend two of them. It shocked me that she believed I had intentions to hurt her, which is not correct.

I cherish our friendship and would never harm her emotionally. I had no idea Rosie was her relative, nor the young man in the picture. I don't communicate with men under 50. To put it simply, he doesn't capture my interest. I greatly appreciate her friendship and would never jeopardize it.

2022/07/03 Bigger Expectations

I have been working out for six months since January. close to 200 lbs., and I took a stand. Determined to lose weight and get in shape, I examined my body and the scale. I wanted to steer clear of health problems caused by weight gain. Through hard work, I slowly improved intensity and endurance. I am now stronger and more confident at 164 lbs. I am pleased with the hard work.

After breakfast, I left home at 7:30 and returned two hours later for coffee and scrambled eggs. After breakfast I cleaned the house, took out the trash, and took a shower, and then I drove to my home and spent the rest of the day with my kids and ex-wife. We ate pizza and chicken wings, watched a movie, and returned home by 7:00 p.m.

2022/07/04 May the 4th Be with You!

Today is July 4th, and Star Wars fans may understand the title of this entry. I got up as usual at 5:30 a.m., but unlike other days, I didn't get up to exercise. I relaxed in the morning instead. I cleaned the house, then spent the day with my kids in Powder Springs before returning to Dallas, Georgia. I skipped fireworks displays due to feeling vulnerable.

2022/07/06 Uncertain Time

My finances have been plummeting like a wagon with no brakes on the edge of a cliff. It's increasingly difficult to improve the situation with rising prices for everything. I'm fortunate my landlord hasn't raised my rent, unlike new tenants. Despite applying to many part-time jobs, I haven't received any calls.

I never imagined being in such a tough spot, but I'm actively seeking new ways to generate income. Started travel business in March, no earnings yet. I need a new strategy for this situation. I'm posting vacation packages on Facebook.

I am expecting one more thing to help me grow my finances, even if it's challenging. After two years without casting calls, I received an offer for a medical examiner's role on Thursday. I hope this leads to more opportunities, maybe a movie role.

My finances have gone so low that some months I did not know if I was going to make it to the next. How was I going to buy groceries, pay my rent and bills, I turned to food pantries to get groceries and this was so painful,

I've never been in this situation or sought help. Difficult circumstances often necessitate making choices that are out of the ordinary.

I found a local pantry that offered help. I went to pick up food at a pantry a mile from my home in Dallas, Georgia. The pantry was behind the courthouse, down a narrow road in the antique business area of the town.

I went into the office and filled out the paperwork and shortly after that I was asked to drive to the front of the building to the loading zone where volunteers had shopping carts loaded with food.

When I arrived at the area, I opened the back hatch of my car and someone instructed me to pick up the food from the shopping cart.

Looking in the cart, the abundance of food shocked me. I asked if I could choose what I needed and was told it was all for me.

Witnessing such generosity in times of need was truly unbelievable. I felt blessed and my first thought was to thank God; I did not expect so much. Tears started streaming down my face. I was fortunate not to go hungry, thanks to God's intervention.

I began loading the food into the back of my car. A Hyundai Veloster is a compact car with an enormous trunk, and I could fill it with so much food that it lasted me a month.

2022/07/08 The Storm Is Not Over Yet

Stress is difficult to deal with, but remaining hopeful you can overcome any obstacles. I am facing financial uncertainty month to month.

Consolidating all credit cards and loans improved my credit rating significantly. My credit score plummeted and my finances suffered after moving out. In just six months, my bank account balance plummeted from $4,500 to $500, causing depression and fear of homelessness. However, it is not in God's plan for me.

I applied for a small personal loan of $2,500 and was afraid they would deny it. They approved the request, and though it's not a significant amount, it should help me.

Eventually, I ended up at Walmart. While shopping, I realized I had left my phone at the self-serve register. I always keep my shopping list handy while shopping.

I put the phone in my bag but I was so distracted by so many things running through my mind that I instead placed my phone on the side of the register and left it right there,

I worried about never finding my phone and the data it held. The phone will auto-lock in one minute and any unlocking attempt will erase all data.

Due to the hot weather, I went back to Walmart and took my bags to keep my milk and cheese from spoiling. Tears streamed down my face as I explained my dilemma to an associate who directed me to the customer service center.

I quickly walked to the customer service center, where only one person was working and there was a line of six people, making me more worried about getting my phone back. Five minutes in line and another store associate came to the counter, and the line began moving.

As I bowed my head over the shopping cart with my purchases and cried but soon calmed down, it felt like it took a long time, but I was in line for about twelve minutes.

I got to the counter when my turn was up; that was an exhausting moment as I approached the woman behind the counter and told her that I left my phone and described it to her.

My nerves were on high as I saw her walk to a cart a few steps from her to look for a phone in a pink flower case and there it was right on the top. I was relieved that I got my phone back and I once more slumped over my shopping cart and cried a moment of relief as I headed out the door.

I cried a bit once more as tears were still rolling down my face. I didn't want to draw attention, so I worked hard to control my emotions and made it back to my car, and went back home.

2022/07/12 So Many Accomplishments, So Much Uncertainty

For the past couple of days, I have been working hard to create ads for my new business and though my new page is growing in members I have yet to make a single booking, but I remain focused on my development.

Today I worked on creating a new image and loaded it to Facebook and I am getting a lot of likes. I'm just hoping that soon enough I can make my first sale.

I went out this afternoon and walked seven thousand steps and returned home and watched a live feed on Facebook from a friend doing makeup I cried when I saw her using products that I would like to buy, but I don't have money to buy anything.

I can't afford simple makeup items that I have run out of or am nearly running out of, so it made me feel sad.

2022/07/14 Tamara's 1st Latin Women's Business Seminar

I had a good day today, filled with excitement and anticipation. A month ago, I signed up for a business seminar created for Latin businesswomen hosted by the Atlanta Latin Association.

I was worried about being rejected because I'm transgender. Closer to the day, thoughts filled my mind. Just hours before, I emailed asking the important question: Can I come as a transgender woman?

This question may seem ridiculous to most, but it was important to me. Unsure of the reception, I feared exclusion due to the event's focus on women.

It sounds silly, but I was serious. The answer to my question came surprisingly quickly, as if someone expected it. It was simply: Why does it matter?

It was all I needed to prepare for the event. I take a long time to prepare, but I already had an outfit ready and had already shaved early in the day to clean my face before makeup.

I got dressed and did my makeup. I wore black pants with a flower print and a pink top with a zipper. The place is 45 miles from my rental home in Dallas, Georgia.

Google Maps showed it takes one hour and eleven minutes, but it took me almost two hours in heavy traffic prior to my arrival. It rained intensely and I thought I was the last one to arrive, but to my surprise. A woman arrived, her head shielded from rain with a towel.

I looked around my car for my umbrella and though I keep one in my car, there was no umbrella to be found so I had to make a quick run up the stairs to the building entrance and my hair and clothes got wet but not so much, but I was wet.

When I entered, it seemed like the event might have been delayed because of the weather. A young woman greeted me outside of the room.

Seated behind a foldable table, she distributed small notebooks to attendees and provided a registration book for them to complete.

Once I registered, my first run was to the bathroom. After relieving my bladder, I washed my hands and took one last look at myself in the mirror before walking into a room full of women.

Being the only transgender woman in attendance, I was relieved to find no discernible stares directed towards me. I blended in well with these beautiful Latinas, each with their own goals for their business. The event was really good and I met so many women there from several Spanish countries.

I heard interesting stories about various businesses, but as the only representative of a travel business, I had five interested women by the end of the event.

2022/07/15 Day of Rest

Yesterday was filled with excitement and adventure. Early morning as usual, my first mission of the day was to walk. My usual step count is 5-6k, but yesterday I reached nearly 11k.

When I walk, I don't have a specific step or time goal. I don't push myself to do more than I can do, but I encourage myself to push forward even if I feel like I've done enough.

While walking, I encourage myself to keep going. And the farther I walked around the neighborhood I live in, the farther I walked past another side street to a shortcut to home. I'm glad I didn't take that shortcut and kept going.

After my morning walk, I had a couple of calls to make, a few emails to read, and Facebook posts to read or block for soliciting and people asking for personal accounts that I am not sharing with anyone.

By 11:00 a.m. it was time for me to prepare for an interview with Red Lobster at 2:00 p.m. It takes me about an hour to get ready, which includes everything from choosing an outfit to putting on makeup and accessorizing.

It takes time to create an outstanding positive image. I made my appointment, though I was thirty minutes late because Google Maps had me going in circles on the wrong side of the road. I had another event to attend after the interview at a local wine bar called Paint & Sip in Dallas, Georgia.

Upon entering, I befriended a dark-skinned woman, also a first timer. We sat at a table at the end of the small bar with about ten tables. An elderly woman joined us at our table when she couldn't find an empty one.

Four of us, who didn't know each other, met in a new place. We painted rocks, made friends, and had a fantastic two hours. In the end, we became friends, shared phone numbers and Facebook profiles, and hugged each other before leaving. Today I need to rest after an amazing day.

2022/07/17 PFLAG Atlanta

I woke up around 5:30 a.m., my usual time. I sat up on the bed and was browsing my Facebook page. I felt tired from the previous day's busyness and a baby shower.

I was tired and planned to go to church and a support group, but I chose to save gas instead.

I decided to participate in church remotely and then join the PRFLAG Atlanta support group at 2:30 p.m. and that is what I did at 10:00 a.m. I attended the church service on time.

After the service, I quickly prepared myself to go to Chamblee, Georgia, which is about an hour away. I left the house at around 11:30 a.m. wearing blue dress pants and a short sleeve top with printed roses. I accessorized with a nice choke collar that had pink shine stones, and I also wore matching earrings.

I stopped at Chamblee's Walgreens for my prescriptions. At the fueling station for gas and at McDonald's for a sandwich and an ice cold coffee, I ate the 1/4 lb. I continued my journey after leaving the parking lot, eating my sandwich and drinking a cold brew of coffee. I arrived a few minutes late because of the heavy traffic.

2022/07/18 A Slow Day

I'm used to getting up early, even without an alarm. I wake up between 5:30 a.m. and 6:00 a.m. Today I woke up just fifteen minutes before 6:00 a.m., but I felt sleepy and like I didn't have enough energy, so I procrastinated a bit before getting out of bed.

I checked my weight and blood pressure and changed from my pj's to comfortable leggings and a short black sleeve T-shirt and headed out the door by 7:30 a.m. for my morning walk and walked for about one and a half hours, and I spent the rest of the day online creating an ad for my travel business, browsing my Facebook pages, and reading emails.

This is my last week of FMLA, so I called my doctor's office to set up an appointment to get a release letter and the appointment is for tomorrow at 11:45 a.m., after that, I had lunch and worked on my site a bit more, and by 4:30 p.m.

I cooked pasta with pork, tomato sauce, mushrooms, and onions. I had dinner and then planned to go for a walk, but it started raining, so I had to stay indoors.

In Summary

For most of my life, I hid my gender identity, keeping it locked away like a forgotten treasure in a secret closet. The sound of fabric rustling would fill the air as I carefully selected and donned women's clothing, a silent rebellion against the expectations placed upon me. Despite the weight of my efforts, the sight of my reflection would always draw me back, like a moth to a flame, to the comfort and authenticity of feminine attire.

Even though I was married, I felt like an actor on a stage, playing a role that didn't align with my true self. The scent of pretense permeated the air, as I meticulously crafted an illusion to protect those around me. My dedication to my spouse and children was unwavering, like a sturdy oak tree standing tall amidst a storm, providing shelter and support.

My story, like a vast landscape waiting to be explored, holds countless tales and emotions that are yet to be penned in the pages of a book. The journal I've kept holds fragments of my journey, but there is still so much left unwritten, waiting to be immortalized in ink.

Amidst life's ever-changing tides, my enduring spirit remains steadfast, like a lighthouse guiding ships through treacherous waters. I constantly strive to improve, driven by an inner fire that refuses to be extinguished.

When others contemplate my identity, their focus often narrows to the negatives. I am a Latin transgender woman with dreams. But what they fail to see is the vibrant tapestry of positivity, strength, and courage that I embody. Like a majestic tiger, my Chinese zodiac animal, I don't seek an easy path for my dreams. I simply yearn for the knowledge that they are within reach, waiting to be grasped.

Believe in yourself, and the world will witness your inherent value, like a radiant star illuminating the boundless heavens.

www.ingramcontent.com/pod-product-compliance
Lightning Source LLC
Chambersburg PA
CBHW061656120626
46550CB00003B/967